Anti-Inflammatory Diet for Beginners

Nourish Your Body & Fortify Immunity with Over 1400+ Days of Simple Recipes and a Comprehensive 60-Day Meal Plan to Alleviate Inflammation and Improve Gut Health

Copyright Disclaimer
© [2024], [Anthony Olsen]. All rights reserved.

TABLE OF CONTENTS

INTRODUCTION

Welcome to "Anti-Inflammatory Diet for Beginners: Nourish Your Body & Fortify Immunity with Over 1400 Simple Recipes and a Comprehensive 60-Day Meal Plan to Alleviate Inflammation and Improve Gut Health." If you're picking up this book, you might be suffering from unexplained aches, persistent fatigue, or nagging health issues that just won't go away. You're not alone. Millions struggle with inflammation, often without even knowing it.

Inflammation is the body's natural response to injury and infection, a crucial part of healing. But when it goes unchecked, it can lead to chronic illnesses, including heart disease, diabetes, arthritis, and various autoimmune conditions. Fortunately, there is a silver lining: your diet. The foods you eat can either fuel inflammation or help cool it down.

This book is your gateway to transforming your health through the anti-inflammatory diet. It's not just a list of recipes; it's a journey to understand your body and nourish it with what it truly needs. From day one to day sixty and beyond, you will discover how simple changes to your diet can dramatically reduce inflammation and revitalize your life.

But why trust this guide? I've been where you are now—confused, tired, and frustrated by health issues that seemed to have no solution. Through years of research, experimentation, and collaboration with nutrition experts, I've distilled the essential principles of anti-inflammatory eating into this comprehensive guide. My journey was transformative, and I believe yours can be, too.

As you turn the pages, expect to find not just recipes, but a new perspective on food. You'll learn why certain foods are your allies against inflammation and how others, seemingly innocent, can undermine your health. You'll be equipped with the knowledge to make informed choices and the tools to create lasting habits.

The road to better health begins here and now. Embrace the journey, savor each step, and remember: the best time to start was yesterday; the second-best time is today. Let's embark on this transformative journey together.

CHAPTER 1

UNDERSTANDING THE ANTI-INFLAMMATORY DIET

1. INTRODUCTION TO THE ANTI-INFLAMMATORY DIET

Welcome to your journey toward a healthier lifestyle through the anti-inflammatory diet. This diet is not just about losing weight or following a temporary eating plan; it's about making long-term changes to reduce chronic inflammation and enhance your overall well-being.

Inflammation is a natural process that helps your body defend against illness and injury. However, when inflammation becomes chronic, it can lead to various health issues, including heart disease, arthritis, depression, and more. The good news is that the foods you eat can significantly impact your body's inflammatory response.

The anti-inflammatory diet is centered around whole, nutrient-dense foods that naturally reduce inflammation. This dietary approach emphasizes fruits, vegetables, lean proteins, whole grains, and healthy fats, all of which contribute to reduced inflammation levels and improved health.

Adopting this diet can lead to numerous health benefits, including improved heart health, better digestion, enhanced immune function, and increased energy levels. By choosing foods that support your body's natural defenses, you can combat chronic inflammation and set the foundation for a healthier, more vibrant life.

As we delve into the anti-inflammatory diet, remember that this is a guide to better eating habits and overall health. It's about making informed choices that nourish your body and reduce the risk of inflammation-related diseases. Let's embark on this journey together, exploring how simple dietary changes can make a significant difference in your health and quality of life.

2. FOODS TO EMBRACE

One of the pillars of the anti-inflammatory diet is incorporating foods known for their anti-inflammatory properties. These foods not only help reduce inflammation but also provide your body with the nutrients it needs to function optimally. Here are some key food groups and examples to embrace in your anti-inflammatory diet:

- **Fruits and Vegetables:** Loaded with antioxidants, vitamins, and minerals, fruits and vegetables are the cornerstone of the anti-inflammatory diet. Focus on a variety of colors to ensure a wide range of nutrients. Blueberries, strawberries, cherries, oranges, and leafy greens like spinach and kale are particularly beneficial.

- **Omega-3 Fatty Acids:** Foods rich in omega-3 fatty acids are known for their anti-inflammatory effects. Incorporate fatty fish such as salmon, mackerel, and sardines into your diet. Flaxseeds, chia seeds, and walnuts are excellent plant-based sources of omega-3s.

- **Whole Grains:** Whole grains are packed with fiber, which can help lower levels of C-reactive protein, a marker of inflammation in the blood. Choose whole grains like oats, brown rice, quinoa, and barley over refined carbohydrates.

- **Nuts and Seeds:** Almonds, walnuts, and sunflower seeds provide healthy fats, protein, and fiber, all of which can help combat inflammation. They're also a great source of antioxidants and other nutrients beneficial for reducing inflammation.

- **Healthy Fats:** Incorporating healthy fats into your diet is crucial for fighting inflammation. Olive oil, especially extra virgin, contains polyphenols that help reduce inflammatory markers. Avocados are another excellent source of healthy fats and nutrients.

- **Herbs and Spices:** Many herbs and spices offer significant anti-inflammatory benefits. Turmeric, known for its active compound curcumin, is particularly effective. Ginger, garlic, cinnamon, and rosemary are also great choices to flavor your meals while combating inflammation.

Incorporating these foods into your diet can lead to a significant reduction in inflammation and contribute to your overall health and well-being. Start by adding a few servings of fruits and vegetables to every meal, opting for whole grains, and replacing unhealthy fats with their healthier counterparts. Remember, the goal is to make gradual changes that you can maintain over time, leading to a sustainable and beneficial way of eating.

By choosing these anti-inflammatory foods, you're not only reducing the risk of chronic diseases but also enhancing your energy levels, improving your digestion, and promoting optimal health.

The core of the anti-inflammatory diet revolves around incorporating foods known for their ability to reduce inflammation. These foods not only help in combating inflammation but also provide a wealth of nutrients that support overall health and well-being. Here are some key food groups to embrace:

- **Fruits and Vegetables:** These should be the cornerstone of your diet. Rich in antioxidants, vitamins, minerals, and fiber, fruits and vegetables can reduce inflammation markers in the body. Aim for a variety of colors to ensure a broad spectrum of nutrients. Berries, cherries, apples, beets, carrots, leafy greens, and onions are particularly beneficial.

- **Omega-3 Rich Foods:** Omega-3 fatty acids are known for their anti-inflammatory properties. Include sources like salmon, mackerel, sardines, chia seeds, flaxseeds, and walnuts in your diet to help reduce inflammation and support heart and brain health.

- **Whole Grains:** Replace refined grains with whole grains, which are higher in fiber and nutrients. Foods like oats, quinoa, brown rice, and whole wheat help maintain stable blood sugar levels and reduce inflammation.

- **Lean Proteins:** Opt for lean sources of protein such as chicken, turkey, beans, lentils, and tofu. These foods provide the necessary nutrients without the excessive saturated fat that can exacerbate inflammation.

- **Healthy Fats:** Incorporate healthy fats into your diet from sources like olive oil, avocados, and nuts. These fats can help decrease the risk of inflammation-related diseases by reducing overall inflammation levels in the body.

- **Herbs and Spices:** Many herbs and spices, including turmeric, ginger, garlic, and cinnamon, have natural anti-inflammatory properties. Incorporate these into your meals regularly to enhance flavor and reduce inflammation.

By focusing on these anti-inflammatory foods, you can significantly improve your health while enjoying a varied and delicious diet.

3. FOODS TO AVOID

Just as some foods can help reduce inflammation, others can trigger or exacerbate it. Being mindful of these foods and limiting their intake is crucial for managing inflammation and maintaining good health. Here are the main types of foods to avoid or minimize:

- **Processed and Red Meats:** Foods like sausages, bacon, and processed deli meats contain high levels of saturated fats and additives that can increase inflammation. Limit your intake of these meats and opt for leaner protein sources instead.

- **Refined Carbohydrates:** White bread, pastries, and other foods made with refined grains can lead to spikes in blood sugar and insulin levels, contributing to inflammation. Choose whole grains over refined grains whenever possible.

- **Sugary Foods and Beverages:** Sugar-sweetened drinks and snacks can dramatically increase inflammation in the body. Reduce your consumption of sugary foods and opt for natural sweeteners like fruit or honey in moderation.

- **Trans Fats:** Found in some margarines, snack foods, and fried items, trans fats can raise your bad cholesterol levels and lower your good cholesterol levels, leading to inflammation. Read labels carefully and avoid foods containing partially hydrogenated oils.

- **Excessive Alcohol:** While moderate alcohol consumption can have some health benefits, excessive drinking can harm your body and trigger inflammation. Limit your alcohol intake to moderate levels or avoid it altogether.

- **Artificial Additives:** Artificial colors, flavors, and preservatives found in many processed foods can contribute to inflammation. Aim for fresh, whole foods and read labels to avoid unnecessary additives.

By being mindful of these pro-inflammatory foods and reducing their presence in your diet, you can further support your body's natural ability to combat inflammation and promote overall health.

4. IMMUNITY AND GUT HEALTH CONNECTION

The relationship between your gut health and your immune system is a critical aspect of the anti-inflammatory diet and overall wellness. Approximately 70% of the immune system resides in the gut, a fact that highlights the gut's role beyond digestion — it's a central part of your body's defense system.

- **The Role of the Gut in Immunity:**
  The gut is lined with a vast network of immune cells, part of what's known as the gut-associated lymphoid tissue (GALT). This system is responsible for distinguishing between harmless substances and potential threats to the body, helping to trigger an immune response when necessary. An imbalance in the gut's microbiome — the collection of bacteria, viruses, fungi, and other microbes living in your digestive tract — can lead to an overactive immune response, resulting in chronic inflammation.

- **Impact of Diet on Gut Health:**
  What you eat significantly affects the composition of your gut microbiome. Diets high in fiber from fruits, vegetables, and whole grains support the growth of beneficial gut bacteria, which in turn support immune function and reduce inflammation. Conversely, a diet high in processed foods, sugar, and unhealthy fats can promote the growth of harmful bacteria, leading to an imbalance known as dysbiosis. Dysbiosis can contribute to increased gut permeability (sometimes referred to as "leaky gut"), where harmful substances can escape into the bloodstream and trigger an inflammatory response.

- **Probiotics and Prebiotics:**
  Incorporating probiotics and prebiotics into your diet can help balance the gut microbiome and support immune health. Probiotics are beneficial bacteria found in foods like yogurt, kefir, sauerkraut, and other fermented products. Prebiotics, on the other hand, are non-digestible fibers that feed the healthy bacteria in your gut and are found in foods such as garlic, onions, asparagus, and bananas. Together, probiotics and prebiotics can enhance gut health, support immune function, and reduce inflammation.

- **The Anti-Inflammatory Connection:**
  By adopting an anti-inflammatory diet rich in whole, nutrient-dense foods, you support a healthy gut environment, which in turn supports your immune system and helps reduce chronic inflammation. In addition to dietary changes, other lifestyle factors such as regular exercise, adequate sleep, and stress management can also positively impact gut health and, by extension, immunity.

In conclusion, the connection between gut health and immunity is a cornerstone of the anti-inflammatory diet. By nurturing your gut microbiome through the right dietary choices, you can bolster your immune system, reduce inflammation, and enhance your overall health and well-being. As we move forward, remember that taking care of your gut is not just about improving digestion — it's about supporting your body's ability to fight inflammation and disease.

5. IMPLEMENTING THE DIET

Transitioning to an anti-inflammatory diet can be a rewarding journey toward better health and well-being. However, it's important to approach this change gradually and sustainably. Here are some practical steps to help you successfully implement the diet:

- **Start Small:** If the idea of overhauling your entire diet seems overwhelming, begin with small changes. Incorporate more fruits and vegetables into your meals, switch to whole grains, and replace unhealthy fats with healthier alternatives like olive oil or avocado. Small, manageable changes can lead to lasting habits.

- **Plan Your Meals:** Planning ahead can make it easier to stick to your new eating habits. Spend some time each week to plan your meals and snacks. This can help you avoid the temptation of reaching for convenient, processed foods when you're hungry and unprepared.

- **Cook at Home:** Preparing your own meals gives you control over the ingredients and ensures that you're eating foods that align with the anti-inflammatory diet. Experiment with new recipes and flavors to keep your meals exciting and varied.

- **Read Labels:** When shopping for groceries, pay attention to food labels. Avoid products with high levels of added sugars, salt, and unhealthy fats. Instead, choose whole, unprocessed foods as much as possible.

- **Increase Variety:** The anti-inflammatory diet is rich in a variety of foods. Try to include a rainbow of fruits and vegetables in your diet, as different colors represent different nutrients and antioxidants that can help combat inflammation.

- **Stay Hydrated:** Proper hydration is key to reducing inflammation. Aim to drink plenty of water throughout the day, and limit sugary beverages and alcohol, which can contribute to inflammation.

- **Listen to Your Body:** Pay attention to how different foods affect your body and mood. If you notice that certain foods exacerbate inflammation or digestive issues, consider eliminating them from your diet and observe how you feel.

- **Seek Support:** Making dietary changes can be challenging, so don't hesitate to seek support from family, friends, or a healthcare professional. Joining a community or group with similar health goals can provide encouragement and accountability.

- **Be Patient and Flexible:** Remember that transitioning to an anti-inflammatory diet is a process. It's okay to have setbacks, and it's important to be flexible and kind to yourself as you make these changes. Focus on progress, not perfection, and be open to adjusting your approach as needed.

Implementing the anti-inflammatory diet is about more than just food; it's about fostering a healthier lifestyle that supports your body's natural ability to fight inflammation and disease. By taking these steps, you can move toward a more balanced, healthful way of eating that nourishes your body and mind.

6. CONCLUSION

As we conclude Chapter 1, it's important to reflect on the journey you are about to embark upon. The anti-inflammatory diet is more than a set of dietary restrictions; it's a holistic approach to eating that emphasizes nourishing your body with foods that fight inflammation and promote overall health. By understanding the principles laid out in this chapter, you are now equipped with the knowledge to make informed choices that can lead to a more vibrant, healthier life.

Remember, the transition to an anti-inflammatory diet is a personal journey and one that doesn't happen overnight. It's about making gradual, sustainable changes to your eating habits that can have a lasting impact on your health and well-being. It's normal to encounter challenges along the way, but with persistence and a positive mindset, these hurdles can be overcome.

The benefits of following an anti-inflammatory diet extend beyond just reducing inflammation; they include improved energy levels, better digestive health, enhanced immunity, and a reduced risk of chronic diseases. As you begin to implement these dietary changes, listen to your body and be mindful of how different foods affect you. This self-awareness will be invaluable as you continue to refine and adapt your diet to suit your individual needs.

In the upcoming chapters, we will delve deeper into specific anti-inflammatory foods, provide practical tips for meal planning and preparation, and share delicious recipes to help you incorporate these principles into your daily life. Remember, your journey to better health is a marathon, not a sprint. Be kind to yourself, celebrate your successes, and stay committed to your well-being.

Welcome to the path of anti-inflammatory eating. Here's to a healthier, more energetic, and inflammation-free life!

CHAPTER 2

THE SCIENCE BEHIND THE ANTI-INFLAMMATORY DIET

1. INTRODUCTION TO THE ANTI-INFLAMMATORY DIET

Welcome to your journey toward a healthier lifestyle through the anti-inflammatory diet. This diet is not just about losing weight or following a temporary eating plan; it's about making long-term changes to reduce chronic inflammation and enhance your overall well-being.

Inflammation is a natural process that helps your body defend against illness and injury. However, when inflammation becomes chronic, it can lead to various health issues, including heart disease, arthritis, depression, and more. The good news is that the foods you eat can significantly impact your body's inflammatory response.

The anti-inflammatory diet is centered around whole, nutrient-dense foods that naturally reduce inflammation. This dietary approach emphasizes fruits, vegetables, lean proteins, whole grains, and healthy fats, all of which contribute to reduced inflammation levels and improved health.

Adopting this diet can lead to numerous health benefits, including improved heart health, better digestion, enhanced immune function, and increased energy levels. By choosing foods that support your body's natural defenses, you can combat chronic inflammation and set the foundation for a healthier, more vibrant life.

As we delve into the anti-inflammatory diet, remember that this is a guide to better eating habits and overall health. It's about making informed choices that nourish your body and reduce the risk of inflammation-related diseases. Let's embark on this journey together, exploring how simple dietary changes can make a significant difference in your health and quality of life.

2. CURRENT TRENDS IN ANTI-INFLAMMATORY RESEARCH

Recent advancements in anti-inflammatory research have revolutionized our understanding of how diet influences our health. This section will explore key trends and findings that underscore the importance of dietary choices in managing inflammation.

The Gut Microbiome and Inflammation: Cutting-edge research highlights the significant role of the gut microbiome in influencing systemic inflammation. A balanced gut microbiota, fostered by a diet rich in diverse, fiber-filled foods, can help suppress inflammatory responses, while an imbalanced microbiota may exacerbate them. Studies have shown that diets high in fruits, vegetables, and fermented foods promote a healthier microbiome, thereby reducing inflammation.

Anti-Inflammatory Foods: Scientific studies continue to identify specific foods and nutrients with potent anti-inflammatory effects. Foods rich in omega-3 fatty acids (like salmon and flaxseeds), antioxidants (found in berries and green leafy vegetables), and phytonutrients (abundant in spices like turmeric and ginger) have been shown to significantly reduce markers of inflammation in the body.

Lifestyle Factors: Research has expanded beyond diet alone, highlighting how lifestyle factors such as stress, sleep, and physical activity also play crucial roles in controlling inflammation. Regular exercise and adequate sleep have been linked to lower inflammation levels, emphasizing the importance of a holistic approach to inflammation reduction.

Personalized Nutrition: There is a growing trend towards personalized nutrition, acknowledging that individual responses to foods can vary greatly. This personalized approach is supported by research suggesting that tailoring dietary choices to one's unique genetic makeup, microbiome composition, and lifestyle can be more effective in reducing inflammation compared to one-size-fits-all solutions.

Plant-Based Eating: A significant trend in anti-inflammatory eating is the shift towards plant-based diets. Research indicates that plant-based diets, which are naturally high in anti-inflammatory compounds, can lower the risk of chronic diseases associated with inflammation.

By staying informed about these current trends and incorporating this knowledge into your diet, you can take proactive steps towards managing inflammation and improving your overall health. In the next sections, we'll delve into nutritional strategies and expert advice on how to adopt an anti-inflammatory lifestyle.

3. NUTRITIONAL STRATEGIES TO COMBAT INFLAMMATION

Adopting an anti-inflammatory diet involves more than just choosing the right foods; it's about understanding how different nutrients interact with the body's inflammatory processes. Here, we'll explore key nutritional strategies that can help you combat inflammation effectively.

Balance Omega-3 and Omega-6 Fatty Acids: While omega-6 fatty acids are essential, an imbalance favoring omega-6 over omega-3 can lead to inflammation. Aim to balance these fatty acids by reducing the intake of omega-6-rich foods like certain vegetable oils and processed snacks, and increasing omega-3 sources such as fatty fish, walnuts, and flaxseeds.

Increase Antioxidant Intake: Antioxidants counteract oxidative stress, a process that can trigger inflammation. Incorporate a variety of colorful fruits and vegetables into your diet to ensure a broad spectrum of antioxidants, such as vitamins C and E, beta-carotene, and selenium.

Focus on Fiber: High-fiber foods not only promote gut health but also help reduce inflammation. Whole grains, beans, lentils, and a variety of fruits and vegetables are excellent sources of fiber that can support a healthy inflammatory response.

Choose Whole Foods Over Processed: Processed and fast foods often contain additives and high levels of salt and sugar, which can exacerbate inflammation. Opt for whole, unprocessed foods whenever possible to reduce your intake of these inflammatory agents.

Incorporate Anti-Inflammatory Spices: Spices like turmeric, ginger, cinnamon, and garlic not only add flavor to your meals but also possess potent anti-inflammatory properties. Regularly including these spices in your diet can help reduce inflammation and enhance overall health.

Stay Hydrated: Adequate hydration is essential for reducing inflammation. Water helps flush toxins from the body and ensures proper cell function. Aim for at least eight glasses of water a day and more if you are active or live in a hot climate.

By integrating these nutritional strategies into your daily routine, you can significantly impact your body's inflammatory response. It's important to remember that changes won't happen overnight, but consistent application of these principles can lead to noticeable improvements in inflammation and overall health.

4. EXPERT ADVICE ON THE ANTI-INFLAMMATORY DIET

Drawing from the wealth of knowledge provided by nutritionists, dietitians, and medical professionals, this section compiles expert advice on adopting and maintaining an anti-inflammatory diet effectively.

Start with Whole Foods: The foundation of an anti-inflammatory diet is a variety of whole, unprocessed foods. Experts suggest making fruits and vegetables the centrepiece of your meals, complemented by whole grains, lean proteins, and healthy fats.

Moderation is Key: While no single food causes or cures inflammation, balance and moderation are crucial. Experts recommend a balanced plate model: half of your plate filled with fruits and vegetables, a quarter with whole grains, and the remaining quarter with lean protein.

Mindful Eating: Pay attention to your body's signals. Eat slowly and stop when you're full. Mindful eating can help prevent overeating, which is linked to increased inflammation.

Consistency Over Perfection: Adopting an anti-inflammatory diet is a long-term commitment to your health. Experts advise that consistency is more important than perfection. Occasional indulgences are part of life, but they shouldn't derail your overall eating habits.

Personalization: Remember that individual responses to foods vary. What works for one person may not work for another. Tailor your diet to your personal preferences, health conditions, and reactions to different foods.

Inclusion Over Exclusion: Instead of focusing solely on eliminating foods, experts suggest emphasizing the addition of healthy, anti-inflammatory foods to your diet. This positive approach can make dietary changes more sustainable and enjoyable.

Regular Check-ins: Periodically assess how your diet is affecting your health and well-being. Changes in energy levels, mood, and physical symptoms can provide valuable feedback on your dietary choices.

Seek Professional Guidance: If you have specific health issues or dietary needs, consulting with a healthcare provider or a dietitian can provide personalized advice and support.

By following this expert advice, you can navigate the journey toward an anti-inflammatory lifestyle with confidence and clarity. Remember, the goal is to foster a healthier relationship with food that supports your body's natural ability to combat inflammation.

5. THE ROLE OF THE ANTI-INFLAMMATORY DIET IN DISEASE PREVENTION AND MANAGEMENT

Adopting an anti-inflammatory diet impacts more than just short-term health—it plays a significant role in preventing and managing chronic diseases. Here's how an anti-inflammatory approach to eating contributes to long-term health benefits:

Cardiovascular Health: Inflammation is a critical factor in cardiovascular diseases, such as heart disease and stroke. An anti-inflammatory diet, rich in omega-3 fatty acids, fiber, and antioxidants, can help reduce cardiovascular risk factors. This includes lowering high blood pressure, reducing cholesterol levels, and improving arterial health, thereby decreasing the likelihood of heart-related problems.

Diabetes Management: Chronic inflammation is linked to the development of insulin resistance, a condition that often precedes type 2 diabetes. By helping to stabilize blood sugar levels and enhance insulin sensitivity, an anti-inflammatory diet can be a key component in preventing the onset of diabetes and managing the condition for those already diagnosed.

Joint Health and Arthritis: Inflammation directly contributes to the pain, swelling, and stiffness associated with arthritis and other joint conditions. Integrating anti-inflammatory foods into one's diet can alleviate symptoms by reducing the inflammatory response in the body, thereby improving joint function and quality of life.

Mental Health: Recent studies suggest a strong connection between diet-induced inflammation and mental health issues, including depression and anxiety. Nutrients from anti-inflammatory foods may support brain health, aiding in the reduction of mental health symptoms and contributing to overall emotional well-being.

Immune Function and General Well-being: A consistent anti-inflammatory diet supports the immune system by preventing an overactive inflammatory response, which can protect the body against a variety of illnesses. Furthermore, improving overall diet quality through anti-inflammatory foods can lead to enhanced vitality and well-being.

The anti-inflammatory diet is more than a means of reducing inflammation—it's a holistic approach to better health that can significantly reduce the risk of various chronic conditions. By making informed dietary choices, individuals can support their body's natural defense mechanisms, leading to a healthier, more balanced life. This lifestyle shift, grounded in scientific research and health principles, underscores the profound impact of diet on disease prevention and overall health management.

6. CONCLUSION: EMBRACING THE ANTI-INFLAMMATORY LIFESTYLE

As we conclude this chapter, remember that the journey to an anti-inflammatory lifestyle is a gradual process of making informed, healthful dietary choices. This approach is not about strict dieting or deprivation but about understanding and implementing a balanced, nutritious eating pattern that reduces inflammation and promotes overall health.

The anti-inflammatory diet's principles are grounded in scientific research and aim to enhance your quality of life by preventing and managing chronic diseases, improving mental and physical well-being, and strengthening your immune system. By embracing whole, nutrient-rich foods and minimizing the intake of processed and pro-inflammatory items, you're taking significant steps toward a healthier, more vibrant self.

It's important to note that dietary changes alone might not resolve all health issues, but they can play a crucial role in a holistic approach to health and wellness. Alongside a balanced diet, consider incorporating regular physical activity, adequate sleep, stress management techniques, and routine medical check-ups to fully support your anti-inflammatory lifestyle.

As you move forward, remember that everyone's journey is unique. Listen to your body, be patient with yourself, and make adjustments as needed. The transition to an anti-inflammatory diet is a personal one, filled with discovery and learning about what best supports your body and health.

The principles laid out in this chapter provide a foundation for a life less inflamed, more energized, and richly nourished. As you continue to explore and apply these principles, you'll not only navigate your path to reduced inflammation but also toward a more balanced, healthful future.

CHAPTER 3

PREPARATIONS FOR 60-DAY MEAL PLAN

1. INTRODUCTION TO THE 60-DAY PLAN

Embarking on a journey towards better health through diet can be both exciting and daunting. This 60-day meal plan is designed to introduce you to the anti-inflammatory lifestyle, guiding you step by step as you discover nutritious foods that nourish your body and reduce inflammation. The goal of this plan isn't just to provide temporary relief or quick fixes but to foster sustainable eating habits that you can carry beyond the next two months.

This comprehensive guide is structured to gradually integrate anti-inflammatory foods into your diet while reducing the intake of pro-inflammatory ones. Each week, you'll focus on incorporating certain types of foods and recipes that build upon the previous week's lessons and experiences, allowing your body to adjust naturally.

Before diving into the meal plan, it's essential to prepare both mentally and physically. Embrace the mindset that this plan is not a diet in the traditional sense but a new approach to eating that prioritizes your health and well-being. Be ready to experiment with new flavors, ingredients, and cooking methods, and remember that flexibility and patience are key. Every individual's body responds differently, so feel free to adapt the plan to suit your tastes, dietary restrictions, and nutritional needs.

As you embark on this 60-day journey, keep an open mind and consider this an opportunity to learn about your body, discover new foods, and understand the profound impact nutrition has on your overall health. By the end of these two months, the goal is for you to feel empowered, rejuvenated, and equipped with the knowledge to continue leading an anti-inflammatory lifestyle.

In the following sections, we'll provide you with everything you need to get started: from preparation and mindset tips to weekly meal plans and shopping lists, all designed to support you on this transformative journey.

2. GETTING STARTED: PREPARATION AND MINDSET

Before you jump into the meal plan, it's crucial to prepare both your kitchen and your mindset. Here are some steps to ensure you're ready to start this journey:

Mindset Shift: Begin by shifting your perspective towards viewing food as a form of medicine for your body. Understand that the choices you make can significantly impact your health and well-being. Commit to this plan not as a temporary diet but as a step towards a lifelong journey of healthier eating habits.

Set Realistic Goals: Identify clear, achievable goals for the next 60 days. Whether it's reducing symptoms of a particular health condition, improving energy levels, or simply feeling better overall, having specific objectives will help keep you motivated.

Clean Out Your Kitchen: Remove temptations and pro-inflammatory foods from your pantry, fridge, and freezer. This might include processed foods, sugary snacks, and items high in unhealthy fats. By clearing out these foods, you'll make room for healthier alternatives.

Stock Up on Essentials: Fill your kitchen with anti-inflammatory staples, including a variety of fruits and vegetables, whole grains, lean proteins, and healthy fats like olive oil and avocados. Consider also investing in quality spices and herbs, which can add flavor and anti-inflammatory benefits to your meals.

Plan Your Meals: Take some time each week to plan your meals and snacks. This can help prevent last-minute decisions that might lead to unhealthy choices. Use the meal plans provided in this chapter as a guide, but feel free to adapt them based on your preferences and needs.

Invest in Food Storage: Having a set of quality food storage containers can make meal prep easier and more efficient. Prepare portions of your meals in advance and store them properly to maintain freshness and reduce food waste.

Seek Support: Inform your family or housemates about your plan and, if possible, encourage them to join you. Having support can make the transition easier and more enjoyable. Additionally, consider joining online communities or forums for extra motivation and advice.

Embrace Flexibility and Patience: Understand that there will be ups and downs throughout this journey. Be patient with yourself and flexible in your approach. If you slip up or face challenges, assess what went wrong and how you can address it moving forward without harsh self-judgment.

By properly preparing yourself and your environment, you'll set a solid foundation for success over the next 60 days. Remember, this is about making sustainable changes that benefit your health in the long term. With the right mindset and preparation, you can navigate this journey with confidence and ease.

3. WEEKLY FOCUS AREAS

To make your transition to an anti-inflammatory diet both manageable and effective, we've divided the 60-day plan into weekly focus areas. Each week introduces new foods and habits designed to reduce inflammation and improve your health, building gradually to incorporate a wide range of anti-inflammatory foods into your diet.

Week 1: Introduction to Whole Foods
- Focus: Replace processed foods with whole, unprocessed options.
- Key Foods: Fresh fruits, vegetables, whole grains.
- Goal: Begin to notice how whole foods affect your energy levels and overall well-being.

Week 2: Incorporating Anti-Inflammatory Fats
- Focus: Introduce more omega-3 fatty acids and reduce omega-6 fatty acid intake.
- Key Foods: Fatty fish, walnuts, flaxseeds, olive oil.
- Goal: Start to incorporate these foods into meals, noticing any changes in how you feel.

Week 3: Optimizing Gut Health
- Focus: Improve gut health with fiber-rich foods and probiotics.
- Key Foods: Fermented foods, high-fiber fruits and vegetables, whole grains.

- Goal: Enhance digestion and start to establish a healthier gut microbiome.

Week 4: Reducing Added Sugars
- Focus: Identify and reduce sources of added sugars in your diet.
- Key Foods: Focus on natural sources of sweetness like fruit.
- Goal: Decrease sugar cravings and stabilize blood sugar levels.

Week 5: Adding Colourful Vegetables and Fruits
- Focus: Increase intake of a variety of colourful produce.
- Key Foods: Berries, leafy greens, beets, carrots, and bell peppers.
- Goal: Boost antioxidant intake and enjoy a range of flavours and textures.

Week 6: Integrating Healing Spices
- Focus: Use spices and herbs to add flavour and anti-inflammatory properties.
- Key Foods: Turmeric, ginger, garlic, cinnamon.
- Goal: Familiarize yourself with the flavours and health benefits of these spices.

Week 7: Mindful Eating and Hydration
- Focus: Practice mindful eating and ensure adequate hydration.
- Key Foods: Continue with varied, anti-inflammatory foods; focus also on water and herbal teas.
- Goal: Improve hydration, and develop a more mindful relationship with food.

Week 8: Review and Reflect
- Focus: Assess your progress and make adjustments as needed.
- Key Foods: Personal favorites from the previous weeks.
- Goal: Identify what works best for you and plan how to continue beyond the 60 days.

Each week builds on the last, allowing you to gradually adjust to new eating habits and understand how different foods and practices affect your body and mind. Remember, this plan is flexible—feel free to adapt it to suit your individual needs and preferences.

4. WEEKLY MEAL PLANS

To help you implement the weekly focus areas, we've created detailed meal plans for each week. These plans are designed to be flexible and adaptable to your personal preferences and dietary needs. In Chapter 14 we provide recipes for each week meal plan.

Week 1: Introduction to Whole Foods
- **Breakfast:** Oatmeal topped with fresh berries and a sprinkle of flaxseed.
- **Lunch:** Grilled chicken salad with mixed greens, vegetables, and olive oil dressing.
- **Dinner:** Baked salmon with quinoa and steamed broccoli.
- **Snacks:** Carrot sticks with hummus, apple slices with almond butter.

Week 2: Incorporating Anti-Inflammatory Fats
- **Breakfast:** Smoothie with spinach, avocado, banana, and chia seeds.
- **Lunch:** Turkey and avocado wrap with whole grain tortilla and mixed greens.
- **Dinner**: Grilled mackerel with sweet potato and sautéed kale.
- **Snacks:** Walnuts, Greek yogurt with honey and almonds.

Week 3: Optimizing Gut Health
- **Breakfast:** High-fiber cereal with almond milk and sliced banana.
- **Lunch:** Lentil soup with a side salad and whole grain roll.
- **Dinner:** Stir-fried tofu with mixed vegetables and brown rice.
- **Snacks:** Kefir, sliced pear with cottage cheese.

Week 4: Reducing Added Sugars
- **Breakfast:** Greek yogurt with mixed berries and unsweetened granola.
- **Lunch:** Grilled chicken Caesar salad (no croutons) with a vinaigrette dressing.
- **Dinner:** Beef stir-fry with bell peppers, broccoli, and a side of quinoa.
- **Snacks:** Sliced cucumber with guacamole, fresh cherries.

Week 5: Adding Colorful Vegetables and Fruits
- **Breakfast:** Vegetable omelette with spinach, tomatoes, and onions.
- **Lunch:** Quinoa salad with beets, carrots, and a lemon-olive oil dressing.
- **Dinner:** Baked cod with a side of mixed roasted vegetables.
- **Snacks:** Mixed berries, bell pepper slices with hummus.

Week 6: Integrating Healing Spices
- **Breakfast:** Turmeric and ginger-infused oatmeal with apple slices.
- **Lunch:** Chicken curry with mixed vegetables and a side of basmati rice.
- **Dinner:** Chili made with lean ground turkey, beans, and cumin.
- **Snacks:** Cinnamon-spiced almonds, sliced pineapple.

Week 7: Mindful Eating and Hydration
- **Breakfast:** Chia pudding with mixed fruit and a drizzle of honey.
- **Lunch:** Grilled salmon salad with a variety of fresh greens and cucumber.
- **Dinner:** Roasted chicken with asparagus and sweet potatoes.
- **Snacks:** Sliced watermelon, celery sticks with almond butter.

Week 8: Review and Reflect
- **Breakfast:** Your favorite breakfast from the past seven weeks.
- **Lunch:** Your favorite lunch from the past seven weeks.
- **Dinner:** Your favorite dinner from the past seven weeks.
- **Snacks:** Your favorite snacks from the past seven weeks.

Each meal plan is just a guide; feel free to swap meals from different days or weeks, substitute ingredients to suit your taste and dietary restrictions, and adjust portion sizes according to your hunger and fullness cues.

5. WEEKLY SHOPPING LISTS

To simplify your meal preparation, each week comes with a shopping list that corresponds to the meal plan. Here's an example for Week 1:

- Fresh Produce: Spinach, berries, avocados, mixed greens, broccoli, bell peppers, bok choy
- Proteins: Chicken breast, salmon, tofu, lentils
- Grains: Quinoa, whole-grain bread, brown rice, oatmeal
- Fats: Walnuts, olive oil, flaxseeds

- Miscellaneous: Herbal teas, spices (turmeric, ginger, garlic, cinnamon)

Organize your shopping list by category to make your grocery shopping more efficient. You can also add or remove items based on what you already have at home.

To make the most of your time and ensure you stick to your meal plan, consider these meal prep tips:

- **Batch Cooking:** Prepare larger portions of meals like soups, stews, or grains at the beginning of the week. Store them in the fridge or freezer for easy, quick meals on busy days.
- **Chop in Advance:** Wash and chop your vegetables and fruits after shopping. Store them in clear containers in the fridge for easy access when cooking.
- **Plan for Leftovers:** Cook once, eat twice. Plan meals that will give you leftovers for lunch the next day or can be repurposed in a different meal.
- **Use Time-Saving Tools:** Utilize kitchen tools like slow cookers, pressure cookers, or blenders to make meal prep quicker and easier.
- **Pre-pack Snacks:** Portion out snacks like nuts, seeds, or cut-up vegetables into individual servings for a quick grab-and-go option.

By planning ahead and incorporating these meal prep strategies, you can save time, reduce stress, and ensure you have healthy, anti-inflammatory meals ready to go throughout the week.

6. MEAL PREP TIPS AND STRATEGIES

Successful implementation of the anti-inflammatory diet is significantly enhanced by effective meal prep. Here are some strategies to ensure your meal preparation is both efficient and aligned with your dietary goals:

Organize Your Kitchen: A well-organized kitchen space can make meal prep more straightforward and less time-consuming. Keep your ingredients, utensils, and cooking equipment within easy reach. Label your spices, arrange your pantry, and declutter your countertops to create a more functional and enjoyable cooking environment.

Schedule Your Prep Time: Set aside specific times each week for meal planning and preparation. Many find that doing a bulk of the prep work on the weekend saves time during the busier weekdays. By establishing a routine, you'll ensure consistent and stress-free meal prep.

Cook in Batches: Batch cooking is a time-saver. Prepare large quantities of staple items like grains, proteins, and vegetables at the start of the week. Store them in the fridge or freezer, so they're ready to be used in various meals throughout the week.

Embrace Simplicity: Not every meal needs to be a gourmet endeavor. Simple dishes often mean fewer ingredients and less time spent cooking, without sacrificing nutritional value. Find a few go-to recipes that are both easy to prepare and align with the anti-inflammatory diet.

Use Leftovers Wisely: Plan meals so that leftovers can be easily transformed into new dishes. For example, leftover roasted vegetables can be added to salads, omelettes, or wraps. This approach minimizes waste and maximizes the variety of your meals.

Pre-Cut Vegetables and Fruits: Wash, chop, and store vegetables and fruits right after grocery shopping. Having these ready to use makes it more likely you'll reach for them when you need a quick snack or are preparing a meal.

Invest in Quality Storage Containers: Good-quality, airtight storage containers are crucial for keeping your prepped ingredients and meals fresh. Consider investing in glass containers, which are durable and can go from fridge to oven for easy reheating.

Stay Flexible: While planning is crucial, be flexible with your meal prep and eating. Life can be unpredictable, so it's important to adapt as needed without stressing too much about sticking rigidly to your meal plan.

Involve Family or Roommates: If possible, involve your household in the meal prep process. Not only can this make the work lighter and more enjoyable, but it also helps to encourage a shared commitment to healthier eating.

By incorporating these meal prep tips and strategies into your routine, you can significantly reduce the stress and time associated with cooking daily meals. More importantly, you'll be more likely to stick with the anti-inflammatory diet, knowing that you have nutritious and delicious meals readily available.

7. TRACKING PROGRESS AND ADJUSTMENTS

As you navigate through the 60-day meal plan, monitoring your progress and making necessary adjustments is crucial for maximizing the benefits of an anti-inflammatory diet. Here are strategies to effectively track your journey and tailor the diet to your individual needs:

Maintain a Food and Symptom Diary: Keep a daily record of the foods you consume and any symptoms you experience. Note changes in energy levels, digestion, sleep quality, mood, and any inflammatory symptoms such as joint pain or skin conditions. Over time, you may begin to notice patterns that can help identify which foods are beneficial and which may be triggering negative responses.

Set Regular Check-in Points: Designate specific times (e.g., every two weeks) to formally review your progress. Assess changes in your symptoms, overall well-being, and adherence to the meal plan. This regular self-assessment can provide motivation and insight into the effectiveness of your dietary choices.

Listen to Your Body: Pay close attention to how your body reacts to different foods and adjustments in the meal plan. Everyone's body is different, and what works for one person may not work for another. Use the feedback your body gives you to guide your dietary choices.

Adjust Based on Feedback: If you notice certain foods worsen your symptoms or don't agree with you, consider eliminating them from your diet. Conversely, if you find particular foods or habits particularly beneficial, try to incorporate them more frequently.

Seek Professional Guidance: If you're unsure about your progress or how to make adjustments, consider consulting with a healthcare professional or a registered dietitian. They can provide personalized advice and support to help you navigate challenges and refine your diet based on your health status and goals.

Celebrate Improvements: Recognize and celebrate any improvements in your health, no matter how small they may seem. Positive changes, whether it's reduced pain, better sleep, or more energy, are signs that your anti-inflammatory diet is making a difference.

Plan for Long-Term Success: As you near the end of the 60-day plan, start thinking about how you can maintain and build upon the healthy habits you've developed. Consider which changes you can realistically sustain over the long term and how you can continue to incorporate anti-inflammatory eating into your daily life.

By actively tracking your progress and being willing to make adjustments, you can ensure that your anti-inflammatory diet remains tailored to your unique needs and continues to support your health and well-being well beyond the initial 60 days.

8. OVERCOMING CHALLENGES AND STAYING MOTIVATED

Embarking on a new diet and lifestyle can come with its set of challenges, but overcoming these obstacles is crucial for long-term success. Here's how to stay motivated and address common hurdles:

Dealing with Cravings: Cravings for sugary, processed, or other pro-inflammatory foods can be a significant challenge. To combat this, ensure you're eating balanced meals that keep you satiated, incorporate healthy snacks, and find wholesome substitutes that satisfy your cravings without derailing your progress.

Social Situations and Peer Pressure: Eating out or attending social events can pose challenges to sticking with your anti-inflammatory diet. Plan ahead by reviewing restaurant menus online, suggesting eateries with healthier options, or bringing your own dishes to gatherings. Don't be afraid to communicate your dietary needs to friends and family; most will be supportive once they understand your health goals.

Time Management and Meal Prep: Finding time to shop, cook, and meal prep can be daunting. Streamline your meal prep process by batching tasks, using simple recipes, and cooking in bulk. Remember, it's okay to seek shortcuts that don't compromise the quality of your diet, like using pre-chopped vegetables or canned beans.

Staying Motivated: Motivation can wane, especially if you're not seeing immediate results. Keep yourself motivated by setting small, achievable goals, celebrating your successes, and reminding yourself of the reasons you started this journey. Visualizing the long-term health benefits can also help maintain your drive.

Handling Setbacks: Everyone experiences setbacks. When they occur, treat them as learning opportunities rather than failures. Assess what led to the setback, and strategize ways to prevent similar situations in the future. Most importantly, be kind to yourself and recognize that progress is not always linear.

Seeking Support: Don't go it alone. Having a support system, whether it's friends, family, online communities, or a healthcare professional, can provide encouragement and accountability. Sharing experiences, challenges, and successes with others on similar paths can be incredibly motivating.

Remembering Your "Why": Keep in mind the reasons you started the anti-inflammatory diet—whether it's improving your health, reducing pain, or feeling more energetic. When challenges arise, revisiting your "why" can reignite your motivation and help you stay on track.

By acknowledging these challenges and employing strategies to overcome them, you can maintain your commitment to an anti-inflammatory lifestyle and continue working toward your health and wellness goals. Remember, every step forward, no matter how small, is progress.

9. CONCLUSION: MOVING FORWARD AFTER THE 60 DAYS

Congratulations on completing the 60-day journey towards an anti-inflammatory lifestyle. This milestone is just the beginning of a continuous journey towards improved health and well-being. As you move forward, it's important to carry forward the lessons, habits, and insights you've gained. Here's how you can continue to build on your success and maintain an anti-inflammatory lifestyle:

Reflect on Your Journey: Take time to reflect on the past 60 days. Acknowledge the changes you've made, both big and small, and consider how these changes have impacted your health, mood, and overall well-being. Understanding what worked well and what challenges you faced can guide your future choices.

Set New Goals: Based on your experiences, set new health and dietary goals for yourself. These could range from trying new anti-inflammatory foods each week, to incorporating more physical activity into your routine, or even exploring stress reduction techniques. Setting goals will help keep you motivated and focused on maintaining a healthy lifestyle.

Continue Learning: The world of nutrition and health is always evolving. Continue to educate yourself about the anti-inflammatory diet and related health topics. Stay curious and open to new information, and consider how emerging research can inform and enhance your dietary choices.

Make It Sustainable: For lasting change, it's crucial that your anti-inflammatory eating habits are sustainable. Continue to find recipes, foods, and meal prep strategies that fit your lifestyle and preferences. Remember, the best diet is the one that you can stick to in the long run.

Build a Support Network: Maintain or seek out support from friends, family, healthcare professionals, or online communities. Sharing your experiences, exchanging recipes, and celebrating milestones with others can provide encouragement and make the journey more enjoyable.

Listen to Your Body: Pay close attention to how your body responds as you continue with an anti-inflammatory lifestyle. Adjust your diet and lifestyle choices based on what makes you feel your best. Remember, this is a personal journey, and what works for someone else may not work for you.

Be Kind to Yourself: Embrace a mindset of self-compassion throughout your continued journey. There will be ups and downs, but each experience provides an opportunity for growth and learning. Treat yourself with kindness and remember that every step forward, no matter how small, is a positive move towards better health.

As you move forward after the 60 days, remember that adopting an anti-inflammatory lifestyle is a lifelong journey, not a destination. Continue to embrace the principles of anti-inflammatory eating, stay committed to your health, and enjoy the benefits of a balanced, nutrient-rich diet. Here's to your continued success and a future filled with health, vitality, and happiness.

CHAPTER 4

BREAKFAST RECIPES

1. Anti-Inflammatory Turmeric Oatmeal

INGREDIENTS:

- 1 cup rolled oats
- 2 cups almond milk
- 1 tsp turmeric powder
- 1/2 tsp cinnamon
- 1 tbsp chia seeds
- 1 apple, chopped
- 1 tbsp honey (or maple syrup for vegans)
- A pinch of salt

DIRECTIONS:

- In a pot, combine rolled oats, almond milk, turmeric, cinnamon, and a pinch of salt. Bring to a boil, then simmer for 5-7 minutes, stirring occasionally.
- Stir in chia seeds and chopped apple. Cook for another 2-3 minutes.
- Serve hot, drizzled with honey or maple syrup.

🔔 NUTRITIONAL INFORMATION (PER SERVING):

Calories: 320

Fat: 7g

Carbohydrates: 55g

Fiber: 9g

Protein: 10g

2. Berry Anti-Inflammatory Smoothie

INGREDIENTS:

- 1 cup mixed berries (blueberries, strawberries, raspberries)
- 1 banana
- 1 cup spinach leaves
- 1 tbsp flaxseed meal
- 1 cup unsweetened almond milk
- 1/2 tsp vanilla extract

DIRECTIONS:

- Combine all ingredients in a blender.
- Blend on high until smooth.
- Serve immediately.

🔔 NUTRITIONAL INFORMATION (PER SERVING):

Calories: 280

Fat: 4g

Carbohydrates: 53g

Fiber: 11g

Protein: 8g

3. Ginger-Infused Avocado Toast

INGREDIENTS:

- 2 slices whole-grain bread
- 1 ripe avocado
- 1/2 tsp grated ginger
- 1 tbsp lemon juice
- Salt and pepper to taste
- 1/2 tsp red pepper flakes (optional)

DIRECTIONS:

1. Toast the whole-grain bread to your liking.
2. In a bowl, mash the avocado with grated ginger, lemon juice, salt, and pepper.
3. Spread the avocado mixture on the toasted bread.
4. Sprinkle with red pepper flakes if desired.

 **NUTRITIONAL INFORMATION (PER SERVING):**

Calories: 300

Fat: 20g

Carbohydrates: 29g

Fiber: 13g

Protein: 9g

4. Anti-Inflammatory Breakfast Bowl

INGREDIENTS:

- 1/2 cup cooked quinoa
- 1 cup spinach leaves, sautéed
- 1/2 cup cherry tomatoes, halved
- 1/4 cup red bell pepper, diced
- 1/4 cup cucumber, sliced
- 1/4 avocado, sliced
- 1 egg, poached or boiled
- 1 tbsp olive oil
- Salt and pepper to taste

DIRECTIONS:

1. In a bowl, arrange the cooked quinoa as a base.
2. Top with sautéed spinach, cherry tomatoes, bell pepper, cucumber, and avocado slices.
3. Add a poached or boiled egg on top.
4. Drizzle with olive oil and season with salt and pepper.

NUTRITIONAL INFORMATION (PER SERVING):

Calories: 400

Fat: 22g

Carbohydrates: 36g

Fiber: 8g

Protein: 14g

5. Chia Seed Pudding with Mixed Berries

INGREDIENTS:

- 1/4 cup chia seeds
- 1 cup coconut milk
- 1/2 tsp vanilla extract
- 1 tbsp maple syrup
- 1/2 cup mixed berries (fresh or frozen)

DIRECTIONS:

1. In a bowl, mix chia seeds, coconut milk, vanilla extract, and maple syrup. Stir well.
2. Refrigerate for at least 4 hours or overnight until it thickens.
3. Serve topped with mixed berries.

🍽 NUTRITIONAL INFORMATION (PER SERVING):

Calories: 280

Fat: 19g

Carbohydrates: 24g

Fiber: 10g

Protein: 5g

6. Spinach and Mushroom Egg Muffins

INGREDIENTS:

- 6 eggs
- 1 cup chopped spinach
- 1/2 cup diced mushrooms
- 1/4 cup diced onions
- Salt and pepper to taste
- 1/4 tsp garlic powder

DIRECTIONS:

1. Preheat oven to 350°F (175°C). Grease a muffin tin with a little olive oil.
2. In a bowl, whisk the eggs and season with salt, pepper, and garlic powder.
3. Stir in the spinach, mushrooms, and onions.
4. Pour the mixture into the muffin tin and bake for 20-25 minutes, until set.
5. Let cool for a few minutes before serving.

🍽 NUTRITIONAL INFORMATION (PER SERVING):

Calories: 90

Fat: 6g

Carbohydrates: 2g

Fiber: 0.5g

Protein: 6g

7. Almond Butter and Banana Toast

INGREDIENTS:

- 2 slices of whole-grain bread
- 2 tbsp almond butter
- 1 banana, sliced
- 1/2 tsp cinnamon
- 1 tsp honey (optional)

DIRECTIONS:

1. Toast the bread slices to your preference.
2. Spread almond butter evenly on each slice.
3. Top with banana slices and sprinkle with cinnamon.
4. Drizzle with honey if desired.

🛎 NUTRITIONAL INFORMATION (PER SERVING):

Calories: 330

Fat: 18g

Carbohydrates: 36g

Fiber: 7g

Protein: 10g

8. Anti-Inflammatory Breakfast Skillet

INGREDIENTS:

- 1 tbsp olive oil
- 1 small sweet potato, diced
- 1/2 bell pepper, diced
- 1/2 zucchini, diced
- 2 cups spinach
- 2 eggs
- Salt and pepper to taste
- 1/4 tsp paprika

DIRECTIONS:

1. Heat olive oil in a skillet over medium heat. Add sweet potato and cook until beginning to soften.
2. Add bell pepper and zucchini; cook until vegetables are tender.
3. Stir in spinach until wilted. Make two wells in the vegetables and crack an egg into each.
4. Cover and cook until eggs are set to your liking. Season with salt, pepper, and paprika.
5. Serve hot from the skillet.

🛎 NUTRITIONAL INFORMATION (PER SERVING):

Calories: 320

Fat: 18g

Carbohydrates: 27g

Fiber: 6g

Protein: 14g

9. Avocado and Egg Breakfast Salad

INGREDIENTS:

- 2 cups mixed greens (spinach, arugula, kale)
- 1 medium avocado, sliced
- 2 hard-boiled eggs, sliced
- 1/4 cup cherry tomatoes, halved
- 2 tbsp pumpkin seeds
- Dressing: 2 tbsp olive oil, 1 tbsp lemon juice, salt, and pepper to taste

DIRECTIONS:

1. Arrange the mixed greens on a plate. Top with sliced avocado, eggs, and cherry tomatoes.
2. Sprinkle pumpkin seeds over the salad.
3. In a small bowl, whisk together olive oil, lemon juice, salt, and pepper. Drizzle the dressing over the salad before serving.

NUTRITIONAL INFORMATION (PER SERVING):

Calories: 400

Fat: 32g

Carbohydrates: 18g

Fiber: 9g

Protein: 15g

10. Blueberry Almond Overnight Oats

INGREDIENTS:

- 1/2 cup rolled oats
- 3/4 cup almond milk
- 1/2 cup blueberries
- 2 tbsp almond slivers
- 1 tbsp chia seeds
- 1 tbsp maple syrup
- 1/2 tsp vanilla extract

DIRECTIONS:

1. In a jar or bowl, mix together the rolled oats, almond milk, chia seeds, maple syrup, and vanilla extract.
2. Cover and refrigerate overnight.
3. Before serving, top with blueberries and almond slivers.

NUTRITIONAL INFORMATION (PER SERVING):

Calories: 350

Fat: 12g

Carbohydrates: 50g

Fiber: 9g

Protein: 10g

11. Sweet Potato and Kale Hash

INGREDIENTS:

- 1 large sweet potato, diced
- 2 cups chopped kale
- 1 small onion, diced
- 2 tbsp olive oil
- 2 cloves garlic, minced
- Salt and pepper to taste
- 2 eggs (optional)

DIRECTIONS:

1. Heat olive oil in a large skillet over medium heat. Add diced sweet potato and onion; cook until tender.
2. Add minced garlic and chopped kale to the skillet. Continue cooking until the kale has wilted.
3. Season with salt and pepper. Create two wells in the hash and crack an egg into each, if using. Cover and cook until the eggs are set to your desired doneness.
4. Serve hot.

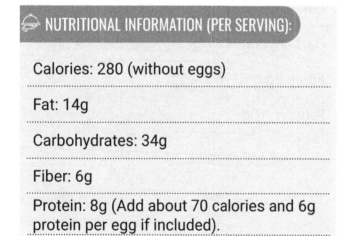

🍽 NUTRITIONAL INFORMATION (PER SERVING):

Calories: 280 (without eggs)

Fat: 14g

Carbohydrates: 34g

Fiber: 6g

Protein: 8g (Add about 70 calories and 6g protein per egg if included).

12. Anti-Inflammatory Smoothie Bowl

INGREDIENTS:

- 1 frozen banana
- 1/2 cup frozen mixed berries
- 1 cup spinach
- 1 tbsp flaxseed meal
- 1/2 avocado
- 3/4 cup coconut water or almond milk
- Toppings: sliced almonds, chia seeds, additional berries

DIRECTIONS:

1. Combine the banana, berries, spinach, flaxseed meal, avocado, and coconut water in a blender. Blend until smooth.
2. Pour into a bowl and add your chosen toppings.

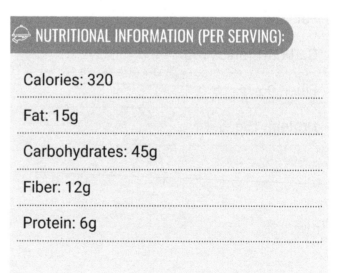

🍽 NUTRITIONAL INFORMATION (PER SERVING):

Calories: 320

Fat: 15g

Carbohydrates: 45g

Fiber: 12g

Protein: 6g

13. Cinnamon Apple Quinoa Breakfast Bowl

INGREDIENTS:

- 1/2 cup quinoa, rinsed
- 1 cup almond milk
- 1 apple, chopped
- 1/2 tsp cinnamon
- 1 tbsp almond butter
- 1 tbsp maple syrup or honey
- 2 tbsp chopped nuts (walnuts, almonds)

DIRECTIONS:

1. Combine quinoa and almond milk in a small pot and bring to a boil. Reduce heat, cover, and simmer for 15 minutes.
2. Stir in chopped apple and cinnamon, cooking for an additional 5 minutes or until quinoa is fully cooked and apples are soft.
3. Serve in a bowl topped with almond butter, maple syrup, and chopped nuts.

🍽 NUTRITIONAL INFORMATION (PER SERVING):

Calories: 380

Fat: 15g

Carbohydrates: 55g

Fiber: 8g

Protein: 10g

14. Avocado Lime Breakfast Smoothie

INGREDIENTS:

- 1 ripe avocado
- 1 cup spinach
- 1 banana
- Juice of 1 lime
- 1 cup coconut water
- 1 tbsp honey or maple syrup (optional)
- Ice cubes (optional)

DIRECTIONS:

1. Place avocado, spinach, banana, lime juice, coconut water, honey, and ice cubes into a blender.
2. Blend until smooth and creamy.
3. Taste and adjust sweetness if necessary, blending again if you add more sweetener.

🍽 NUTRITIONAL INFORMATION (PER SERVING):

Calories: 350

Fat: 12g

Carbohydrates: 50g

Fiber: 9g

Protein: 10g

15. Anti-Inflammatory Breakfast Burrito

INGREDIENTS:

- 2 whole grain or gluten-free tortillas
- 4 eggs, beaten
- 1/2 cup cooked black beans
- 1 avocado, sliced
- 1/2 cup fresh salsa
- 1 cup spinach leaves
- Salt and pepper to taste

DIRECTIONS:

1. Heat a non-stick skillet over medium heat and scramble the eggs seasoned with salt and pepper.
2. Warm the tortillas in a separate pan or microwave.
3. Divide the scrambled eggs between the tortillas, and top with black beans, avocado slices, salsa, and spinach.
4. Roll up the tortillas, folding in the sides to enclose the filling.
5. Serve warm.

🍽 NUTRITIONAL INFORMATION (PER SERVING):

Calories: 450

Fat: 22g

Carbohydrates: 45g

Fiber: 12g

Protein: 20g

16. Ginger Pear Breakfast Bars

INGREDIENTS:

- 1 cup rolled oats
- 1/2 cup almond flour
- 1/4 cup ground flaxseed
- 1 tsp ground ginger
- 1/2 tsp cinnamon
- 1/4 tsp salt
- 2 ripe pears, grated
- 1/4 cup coconut oil, melted
- 1/4 cup maple syrup
- 1 tsp vanilla extract

DIRECTIONS:

1. Preheat the oven to 350°F (175°C) and line an 8-inch square baking pan with parchment paper.
2. In a large bowl, mix together the oats, almond flour, flaxseed, ginger, cinnamon, and salt.
3. Stir in the grated pears, melted coconut oil, maple syrup, and vanilla extract until well combined.
4. Press the mixture firmly into the prepared pan and bake for 25-30 minutes, or until the edges are golden brown.
5. Allow to cool completely before cutting into bars.

🍽 NUTRITIONAL INFORMATION (PER SERVING):

Calories: 220

Fat: 12g

Carbohydrates: 27g

Fiber: 5g

Protein: 5g

These breakfast recipes are designed to provide a balanced start to your day, focusing on anti-inflammatory ingredients that promote health and well-being. Adjust quantities and ingredients based on your personal dietary needs and preferences.

CHAPTER 5

LUNCH RECIPES

1. Quinoa Salad with Roasted Vegetables

INGREDIENTS:

- 1 cup quinoa
- 2 cups mixed vegetables (such as bell peppers, zucchini, and cherry tomatoes)
- 2 tablespoons olive oil
- Salt and pepper to taste
- 1/4 cup chopped fresh parsley
- 1/4 cup crumbled feta cheese (optional)

DIRECTIONS:

1. Preheat the oven to 400°F (200°C).
2. Cook quinoa according to package instructions.
3. Toss mixed vegetables with olive oil, salt, and pepper. Roast for 20-25 minutes until tender.
4. In a large bowl, mix cooked quinoa, roasted vegetables, parsley, and feta cheese (if using).
5. Serve warm or cold.

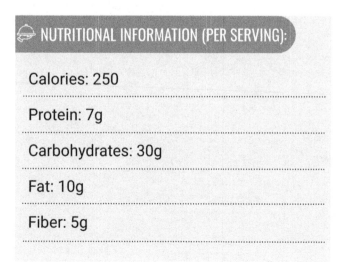

🍽 NUTRITIONAL INFORMATION (PER SERVING):

Calories: 250

Protein: 7g

Carbohydrates: 30g

Fat: 10g

Fiber: 5g

2. Salmon Avocado Salad

INGREDIENTS:

- 8 oz salmon fillet
- 2 cups mixed greens
- 1 avocado, sliced
- 1/4 cup cherry tomatoes, halved
- 1 tablespoon olive oil
- 1 tablespoon lemon juice
- Salt and pepper to taste

DIRECTIONS:

1. Season salmon with salt and pepper. Grill or bake until cooked through.
2. In a large bowl, toss mixed greens, avocado slices, and cherry tomatoes.
3. Top with cooked salmon.
4. Drizzle olive oil and lemon juice over the salad.
5. Serve immediately.

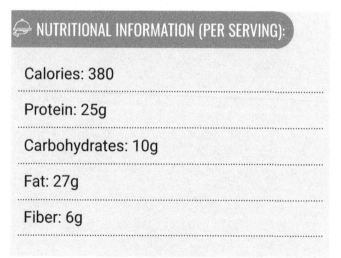

🍽 NUTRITIONAL INFORMATION (PER SERVING):

Calories: 380

Protein: 25g

Carbohydrates: 10g

Fat: 27g

Fiber: 6g

3. Turmeric Chickpea Wraps

INGREDIENTS:

- 1 can (15 oz) chickpeas, drained and rinsed
- 1 teaspoon turmeric powder
- 1/2 teaspoon cumin
- 1/4 teaspoon paprika
- Salt and pepper to taste
- 4 whole grain tortillas
- 1/2 cup hummus
- 1 cup shredded lettuce
- 1/2 cup diced cucumber
- 1/4 cup chopped fresh cilantro

DIRECTIONS:

1. In a skillet, heat chickpeas with turmeric, cumin, paprika, salt, and pepper until warmed through.
2. Spread hummus evenly on each tortilla.
3. Top with chickpeas, shredded lettuce, diced cucumber, and fresh cilantro.
4. Roll up the tortillas tightly.
5. Slice in half and serve.

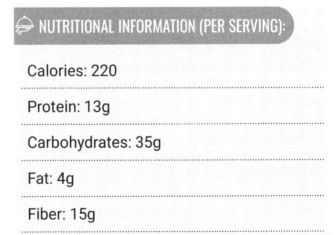

🍽 NUTRITIONAL INFORMATION (PER SERVING):

Calories: 320

Protein: 13g

Carbohydrates: 50g

Fat: 9g

Fiber: 12g

4. Lentil and Vegetable Soup

INGREDIENTS:

- 1 cup dried lentils
- 4 cups vegetable broth
- 1 onion, diced
- 2 carrots, diced
- 2 celery stalks, diced
- 2 cloves garlic, minced
- 1 teaspoon turmeric
- 1 teaspoon ground ginger
- Salt and pepper to taste
- 2 tablespoons olive oil
- Fresh parsley for garnish

DIRECTIONS:

1. In a large pot, heat olive oil over medium heat. Add onions, carrots, celery, and garlic. Cook until vegetables are softened.
2. Add lentils, vegetable broth, turmeric, ginger, salt, and pepper. Bring to a boil, then reduce heat and simmer for 20-25 minutes until lentils are tender.
3. Adjust seasoning if necessary. Serve hot, garnished with fresh parsley.

🍽 NUTRITIONAL INFORMATION (PER SERVING):

Calories: 220

Protein: 13g

Carbohydrates: 35g

Fat: 4g

Fiber: 15g

5. Grilled Chicken Salad with Berry Vinaigrette

INGREDIENTS:

- 8 oz chicken breast
- 4 cups mixed salad greens
- 1/2 cup mixed berries (such as strawberries, blueberries, and raspberries)
- 1/4 cup chopped walnuts
- 2 tablespoons olive oil
- 1 tablespoon balsamic vinegar
- 1 teaspoon honey
- Salt and pepper to taste

DIRECTIONS:

1. Season chicken breast with salt and pepper. Grill until cooked through.
2. In a small bowl, whisk together olive oil, balsamic vinegar, honey, salt, and pepper to make the vinaigrette.
3. In a large bowl, toss mixed salad greens, mixed berries, and chopped walnuts.
4. Slice grilled chicken and place on top of the salad.
5. Drizzle with berry vinaigrette.
6. Serve immediately.

NUTRITIONAL INFORMATION (PER SERVING):

Calories: 380

Protein: 25g

Carbohydrates: 15g

Fat: 25g

Fiber: 5g

6. Sweet Potato and Black Bean Quesadillas

INGREDIENTS:

- 2 medium sweet potatoes, peeled and diced
- 1 can (15 oz) black beans, drained and rinsed
- 1 teaspoon chili powder
- 1/2 teaspoon cumin
- Salt and pepper to taste
- 4 whole grain tortillas
- 1 cup shredded cheddar cheese
- Guacamole and salsa for serving

DIRECTIONS:

1. Boil or steam sweet potatoes until tender. Mash with a fork.
2. In a skillet, heat black beans with chili powder, cumin, salt, and pepper until warmed through.
3. Spread mashed sweet potatoes evenly on two tortillas.
4. Top with black beans and shredded cheddar cheese. Place the remaining tortillas on top.
5. Cook quesadillas in a skillet over medium heat until cheese is melted and tortillas are crispy.
6. Slice into wedges and serve with guacamole and salsa.

NUTRITIONAL INFORMATION (PER SERVING):

Calories: 380

Protein: 18g

Carbohydrates: 50g

Fat: 14g

Fiber: 12g

7. Spinach and Chickpea Salad with Lemon-Tahini Dressing

INGREDIENTS:

- 4 cups baby spinach
- 1 can (15 oz) chickpeas, drained and rinsed
- 1/4 cup sliced red onion
- 1/4 cup sliced almonds
- 2 tablespoons tahini
- 2 tablespoons lemon juice
- 1 tablespoon olive oil
- 1 clove garlic, minced
- Salt and pepper to taste

DIRECTIONS:

1. In a large bowl, combine baby spinach, chickpeas, sliced red onion, and sliced almonds.
2. In a small bowl, whisk together tahini, lemon juice, olive oil, minced garlic, salt, and pepper to make the dressing.
3. Pour the dressing over the salad and toss to coat evenly.
4. Serve immediately.

NUTRITIONAL INFORMATION (PER SERVING):

Calories: 280

Protein: 12g

Carbohydrates: 30g

Fat: 14g

Fiber: 9g

8. Vegetable Stir-Fry with Tofu

INGREDIENTS:

- 1 block (14 oz) firm tofu, cubed
- 2 cups mixed vegetables (such as bell peppers, broccoli, and snap peas)
- 2 tablespoons soy sauce
- 1 tablespoon sesame oil
- 2 cloves garlic, minced
- 1 teaspoon grated ginger
- Cooked brown rice for serving

DIRECTIONS:

1. In a skillet, heat sesame oil over medium heat. Add minced garlic and grated ginger, cook until fragrant.
2. Add cubed tofu to the skillet and cook until golden brown on all sides.
3. Add mixed vegetables and soy sauce to the skillet. Stir-fry until vegetables are tender-crisp.
4. Serve stir-fry over cooked brown rice.

NUTRITIONAL INFORMATION (PER SERVING):

Calories: 320

Protein: 18g

Carbohydrates: 25g

Fat: 16g

Fiber: 6g

9. Mediterranean Chickpea Salad

INGREDIENTS:

- 1 can (15 oz) chickpeas, drained and rinsed
- 1 cucumber, diced
- 1 cup cherry tomatoes, halved
- 1/4 cup diced red onion
- 1/4 cup chopped fresh parsley
- 2 tablespoons olive oil
- 1 tablespoon red wine vinegar
- 1 teaspoon dried oregano
- Salt and pepper to taste
- Crumbled feta cheese for serving (optional)

DIRECTIONS:

1. In a large bowl, combine chickpeas, diced cucumber, cherry tomatoes, diced red onion, and chopped fresh parsley.
2. In a small bowl, whisk together olive oil, red wine vinegar, dried oregano, salt, and pepper to make the dressing.
3. Pour the dressing over the salad and toss to coat evenly.
4. Serve topped with crumbled feta cheese if desired.

NUTRITIONAL INFORMATION (PER SERVING):

Calories: 280

Protein: 9g

Carbohydrates: 30g

Fat: 14g

Fiber: 9g

10. Roasted Vegetable Quinoa Bowl

INGREDIENTS:

- 1 cup quinoa
- 2 cups mixed vegetables (such as bell peppers, eggplant, and carrots)
- 2 tablespoons olive oil
- 1 teaspoon Italian seasoning
- Salt and pepper to taste
- 1/4 cup crumbled goat cheese
- Balsamic glaze for drizzling (optional)

DIRECTIONS:

1. Preheat the oven to 400°F (200°C).
2. Cook quinoa according to package instructions.
3. Toss mixed vegetables with olive oil, Italian seasoning, salt, and pepper. Roast for 20-25 minutes until tender.
4. Divide cooked quinoa among serving bowls.
5. Top with roasted vegetables and crumbled goat cheese.
6. Drizzle with balsamic glaze if desired.
7. Serve warm.

NUTRITIONAL INFORMATION (PER SERVING):

Calories: 320

Protein: 10g

Carbohydrates: 40g

Fat: 14g

Fiber: 8g

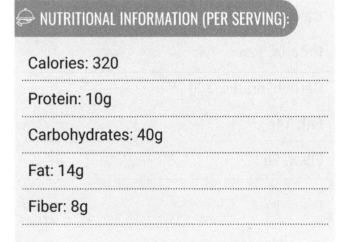

11. Turkey and Avocado Lettuce Wraps

INGREDIENTS:

- 8 oz ground turkey
- 1 teaspoon olive oil
- 1 teaspoon taco seasoning
- 4 large lettuce leaves
- 1 avocado, sliced
- 1/2 cup diced tomatoes
- 1/4 cup shredded cheddar cheese
- Fresh cilantro for garnish

DIRECTIONS:

1. In a skillet, heat olive oil over medium heat. Add ground turkey and taco seasoning. Cook until turkey is browned and cooked through.
2. Arrange lettuce leaves on a plate.
3. Spoon cooked turkey onto each lettuce leaf.
4. Top with avocado slices, diced tomatoes, and shredded cheddar cheese.
5. Garnish with fresh cilantro.
6. Serve immediately.

NUTRITIONAL INFORMATION (PER SERVING):

Calories: 280

Protein: 20g

Carbohydrates: 10g

Fat: 18g

Fiber: 6g

12. Butternut Squash Soup

INGREDIENTS:

- 1 medium butternut squash, peeled and diced
- 1 onion, diced
- 2 carrots, diced
- 2 celery stalks, diced
- 2 cloves garlic, minced
- 4 cups vegetable broth
- 1 teaspoon ground cinnamon
- 1/2 teaspoon ground ginger
- Salt and pepper to taste
- 2 tablespoons coconut cream for garnish (optional)

DIRECTIONS:

1. In a large pot, combine butternut squash, onion, carrots, celery, garlic, vegetable broth, cinnamon, ginger, salt, and pepper.
2. Bring to a boil, then reduce heat and simmer for 20-25 minutes until vegetables are tender.
3. Use an immersion blender to blend soup until smooth.
4. Adjust seasoning if necessary.
5. Serve hot, garnished with coconut cream if desired.

NUTRITIONAL INFORMATION (PER SERVING):

Calories: 220

Protein: 4g

Carbohydrates: 45g

Fat: 4g

Fiber: 8g

13. Mediterranean Quinoa Stuffed Peppers

INGREDIENTS:

- 4 large bell peppers, halved and seeds removed
- 1 cup cooked quinoa
- 1 can (15 oz) chickpeas, drained and rinsed
- 1 cup diced cucumber
- 1 cup cherry tomatoes, halved
- 1/4 cup chopped kalamata olives
- 1/4 cup crumbled feta cheese
- 2 tablespoons olive oil
- 2 tablespoons lemon juice
- 1 teaspoon dried oregano
- Salt and pepper to taste
- Fresh parsley for garnish

DIRECTIONS:

1. Preheat the oven to 375°F (190°C).
2. In a large bowl, combine cooked quinoa, chickpeas, diced cucumber, cherry tomatoes, chopped kalamata olives, crumbled feta cheese, olive oil, lemon juice, dried oregano, salt, and pepper.
3. Stuff each bell pepper half with the quinoa mixture.
4. Place stuffed peppers on a baking sheet lined with parchment paper.
5. Bake for 25-30 minutes until peppers are tender.
6. Garnish with fresh parsley before serving.

🍽 NUTRITIONAL INFORMATION (PER SERVING):

Calories: 280

Protein: 10g

Carbohydrates: 35g

Fat: 12g

Fiber: 9g

14. Chickpea and Spinach Curry

INGREDIENTS:

- 1 tablespoon olive oil
- 1 onion, diced
- 2 cloves garlic, minced
- 1 tablespoon grated ginger
- 1 teaspoon ground cumin
- 1 teaspoon ground coriander
- 1/2 teaspoon turmeric
- 1/4 teaspoon cayenne pepper (optional)
- 1 can (15 oz) chickpeas, drained and rinsed
- 1 can (14 oz) diced tomatoes
- 2 cups fresh spinach leaves
- Salt and pepper to taste
- Cooked brown rice for serving

DIRECTIONS:

1. In a large skillet, heat olive oil over medium heat. Add diced onion, minced garlic, and grated ginger. Cook until onion is softened.
2. Add ground cumin, ground coriander, turmeric, and cayenne pepper (if using). Cook for another minute until fragrant.
3. Stir in chickpeas and diced tomatoes. Simmer for 10-15 minutes.
4. Add fresh spinach leaves and cook until wilted.
5. Season with salt and pepper to taste.
6. Serve curry over cooked brown rice.

🍽 NUTRITIONAL INFORMATION (PER SERVING):

Calories: 320

Protein: 12g

Carbohydrates: 45g

Fat: 10g

Fiber: 12g

15. Grilled Vegetable Panini

INGREDIENTS:

- 1 zucchini, sliced lengthwise
- 1 yellow squash, sliced lengthwise
- 1 red bell pepper, sliced
- 1 yellow bell pepper, sliced
- 4 slices whole grain bread
- 2 tablespoons pesto sauce
- 1/4 cup crumbled goat cheese
- Olive oil spray

DIRECTIONS:

1. Preheat a grill pan or grill over medium-high heat.
2. Spray zucchini, yellow squash, and bell pepper slices with olive oil spray. Grill until tender and slightly charred.
3. Spread pesto sauce on each slice of bread.
4. Layer grilled vegetables and crumbled goat cheese on two slices of bread. Top with the remaining bread slices.
5. Grill the sandwiches in a panini press or skillet until golden brown and cheese is melted.
6. Slice in half and serve hot.

NUTRITIONAL INFORMATION (PER SERVING):

Calories: 280

Protein: 12g

Carbohydrates: 35g

Fat: 10g

Fiber: 8g

16. Asian-Inspired Tofu Salad

INGREDIENTS:

- 1 block (14 oz) extra-firm tofu, cubed
- 4 cups mixed salad greens
- 1 cup shredded carrots
- 1/2 cup sliced cucumber
- 1/4 cup chopped green onions
- 2 tablespoons sesame oil
- 2 tablespoons soy sauce
- 1 tablespoon rice vinegar
- 1 tablespoon honey
- 1 teaspoon grated ginger
- 1 clove garlic, minced
- Sesame seeds for garnish

DIRECTIONS:

1. In a large bowl, combine mixed salad greens, shredded carrots, sliced cucumber, and chopped green onions.
2. In a separate bowl, whisk together sesame oil, soy sauce, rice vinegar, honey, grated ginger, and minced garlic to make the dressing.
3. Heat a skillet over medium-high heat. Add cubed tofu and cook until golden brown on all sides.
4. Add cooked tofu to the salad.
5. Drizzle the dressing over the salad and toss to coat evenly.
6. Garnish with sesame seeds before serving.

NUTRITIONAL INFORMATION (PER SERVING):

Calories: 320

Protein: 18g

Carbohydrates: 25g

Fat: 18g

Fiber: 6g

CHAPTER 6
DINNER RECIPES

1. Baked Salmon with Asparagus

INGREDIENTS:

- 4 salmon fillets (6 oz each)
- 1 lb asparagus, trimmed
- 2 tablespoons olive oil
- 2 cloves garlic, minced
- 1 teaspoon lemon zest
- Salt and pepper to taste
- Fresh dill for garnish

DIRECTIONS:

1. Preheat the oven to 400°F (200°C).
2. Place salmon fillets and asparagus on a baking sheet.
3. In a small bowl, mix olive oil, minced garlic, lemon zest, salt, and pepper.
4. Brush the olive oil mixture over the salmon and asparagus.
5. Bake for 12-15 minutes until salmon is cooked through and asparagus is tender.
6. Garnish with fresh dill before serving.

2. Quinoa Stuffed Bell Peppers

INGREDIENTS:

- 4 large bell peppers, halved and seeds removed
- 1 cup cooked quinoa
- 1 can (15 oz) black beans, drained and rinsed
- 1 cup diced tomatoes
- 1/2 cup corn kernels (fresh or frozen)
- 1/4 cup chopped cilantro
- 1 teaspoon cumin
- 1/2 teaspoon chili powder
- Salt and pepper to taste
- 1/2 cup shredded cheddar cheese (optional)

DIRECTIONS:

1. Preheat the oven to 375°F (190°C).
2. In a large bowl, mix cooked quinoa, black beans, diced tomatoes, corn kernels, chopped cilantro, cumin, chili powder, salt, and pepper.
3. Stuff each bell pepper half with the quinoa mixture.
4. Place stuffed peppers in a baking dish.
5. Cover with foil and bake for 25-30 minutes until peppers are tender.
6. Remove foil, sprinkle shredded cheddar cheese on top (if using), and bake for an additional 5 minutes until cheese is melted.
7. Serve hot.

NUTRITIONAL INFORMATION (PER SERVING):

Calories: 350

Protein: 35g

Carbohydrates: 6g

Fat: 20g

Fiber: 3g

NUTRITIONAL INFORMATION (PER SERVING):

Calories: 320

Protein: 15g

Carbohydrates: 45g

Fat: 8g

Fiber: 12g

3. Lemon Herb Grilled Chicken

INGREDIENTS:

- 4 boneless, skinless chicken breasts
- 2 tablespoons olive oil
- 2 cloves garlic, minced
- 1 teaspoon lemon zest
- 1 tablespoon lemon juice
- 1 teaspoon dried thyme
- 1 teaspoon dried rosemary
- Salt and pepper to taste

DIRECTIONS:

1. In a small bowl, mix olive oil, minced garlic, lemon zest, lemon juice, dried thyme, dried rosemary, salt, and pepper to make the marinade.
2. Place chicken breasts in a shallow dish and pour the marinade over them. Make sure the chicken is evenly coated.
3. Cover and refrigerate for at least 30 minutes.
4. Preheat the grill to medium-high heat.
5. Grill chicken breasts for 6-8 minutes per side until cooked through.
6. Serve hot.

NUTRITIONAL INFORMATION (PER SERVING):

Calories: 280

Protein: 35g

Carbohydrates: 2g

Fat: 14g

Fiber: 0g

4. Lentil and Vegetable Curry

INGREDIENTS:

- 1 cup dried green lentils
- 4 cups vegetable broth
- 1 onion, diced
- 2 carrots, diced
- 2 celery stalks, diced
- 2 cloves garlic, minced
- 1 tablespoon curry powder
- 1 teaspoon ground turmeric
- 1 can (14 oz) diced tomatoes
- Salt and pepper to taste
- Fresh cilantro for garnish

DIRECTIONS:

1. In a large pot, combine dried lentils, vegetable broth, diced onion, diced carrots, diced celery, minced garlic, curry powder, ground turmeric, diced tomatoes, salt, and pepper.
2. Bring to a boil, then reduce heat and simmer for 25-30 minutes until lentils and vegetables are tender.
3. Adjust seasoning if necessary.
4. Serve hot, garnished with fresh cilantro.

NUTRITIONAL INFORMATION (PER SERVING):

Calories: 280

Protein: 15g

Carbohydrates: 50g

Fat: 2g

Fiber: 18g

5. Mediterranean Turkey Meatballs

INGREDIENTS:

- 1 lb lean ground turkey
- 1/2 cup breadcrumbs
- 1/4 cup grated Parmesan cheese
- 1 egg
- 2 cloves garlic, minced
- 1 teaspoon dried oregano
- 1 teaspoon dried basil
- Salt and pepper to taste
- 1 can (14 oz) diced tomatoes
- 1/2 cup chopped fresh parsley
- 1/4 cup crumbled feta cheese

DIRECTIONS:

1. Preheat the oven to 400°F (200°C).
2. In a large bowl, mix ground turkey, breadcrumbs, grated Parmesan cheese, egg, minced garlic, dried oregano, dried basil, salt, and pepper until well combined.
3. Shape the mixture into meatballs and place them on a baking sheet.
4. Bake for 20-25 minutes until meatballs are cooked through and lightly browned.
5. In a skillet, heat diced tomatoes until warmed through.
6. Add cooked meatballs to the skillet and simmer for a few minutes.
7. Serve meatballs topped with chopped fresh parsley and crumbled feta cheese.

🍽 NUTRITIONAL INFORMATION (PER SERVING):

Calories: 280

Protein: 25g

Carbohydrates: 15g

Fat: 12g

Fiber: 3g

6. Garlic Shrimp and Broccoli Stir-Fry

INGREDIENTS:

- 1 lb shrimp, peeled and deveined
- 4 cups broccoli florets
- 2 tablespoons olive oil
- 4 cloves garlic, minced
- 1 tablespoon soy sauce
- 1 tablespoon rice vinegar
- 1 teaspoon honey
- Red pepper flakes to taste
- Sesame seeds for garnish (optional)

DIRECTIONS:

1. Heat olive oil in a large skillet over medium-high heat. Add minced garlic and cook until fragrant.
2. Add shrimp to the skillet and cook until pink and opaque.
3. Add broccoli florets and cook until tender-crisp.
4. In a small bowl, whisk together soy sauce, rice vinegar, honey, and red pepper flakes.
5. Pour the sauce over the shrimp and broccoli. Stir well to coat.
6. Cook for another minute until everything is heated through.
7. Garnish with sesame seeds if desired.
8. Serve hot over cooked brown rice or quinoa.

🍽 NUTRITIONAL INFORMATION (PER SERVING):

Calories: 320

Protein: 30g

Carbohydrates: 15g

Fat: 15g

Fiber: 6g

7. Stuffed Acorn Squash with Turkey and Quinoa

INGREDIENTS:

- 2 acorn squash, halved and seeds removed
- 1 cup cooked quinoa
- 1/2 lb ground turkey
- 1 tablespoon olive oil
- 1 onion, diced
- 2 cloves garlic, minced
- 1 teaspoon dried sage
- 1/2 teaspoon ground cinnamon
- Salt and pepper to taste
- 1/4 cup chopped pecans
- Fresh parsley for garnish

DIRECTIONS:

1. Preheat the oven to 375°F (190°C).
2. Place acorn squash halves on a baking sheet, cut side up.
3. Drizzle with olive oil and season with salt and pepper. Bake for 30 minutes.
4. Meanwhile, in a skillet, heat olive oil over medium heat. Add diced onion and minced garlic, cook until softened.
5. Add ground turkey to the skillet and cook until browned.
6. Stir in cooked quinoa, dried sage, ground cinnamon, salt, pepper, and chopped pecans.
7. Fill each roasted acorn squash half with the turkey-quinoa mixture.
8. Return stuffed squash to the oven and bake for another 20-25 minutes until squash is tender.
9. Garnish with fresh parsley before serving.

NUTRITIONAL INFORMATION (PER SERVING):

Calories: 350

Protein: 20g

Carbohydrates: 35g

Fat: 15g

Fiber: 6g

8. Eggplant and Chickpea Tagine

INGREDIENTS:

- 1 large eggplant, diced
- 1 can (15 oz) chickpeas, drained and rinsed
- 1 onion, diced
- 2 cloves garlic, minced
- 1 can (14 oz) diced tomatoes
- 1/2 cup vegetable broth
- 1 teaspoon ground cumin
- 1 teaspoon ground coriander
- 1/2 teaspoon ground cinnamon
- Salt and pepper to taste
- Fresh cilantro for garnish

DIRECTIONS:

1. In a large pot or tagine, heat olive oil over medium heat. Add diced onion and minced garlic, cook until softened.
2. Add diced eggplant to the pot and cook until slightly browned.
3. Stir in chickpeas, diced tomatoes, vegetable broth, ground cumin, ground coriander, ground cinnamon, salt, and pepper.
4. Bring to a simmer, then reduce heat and cook for 20-25 minutes until eggplant is tender.
5. Adjust seasoning if necessary.
6. Serve hot, garnished with fresh cilantro.

NUTRITIONAL INFORMATION (PER SERVING):

Calories: 280

Protein: 12g

Carbohydrates: 40g

Fat: 8g

Fiber: 12g

9. Turkey and Vegetable Skillet

INGREDIENTS:

- 1 lb ground turkey
- 2 tablespoons olive oil
- 1 onion, diced
- 2 cloves garlic, minced
- 2 carrots, diced
- 2 celery stalks, diced
- 1 bell pepper, diced
- 1 zucchini, diced
- 1 can (14 oz) diced tomatoes
- 1 teaspoon dried oregano
- 1 teaspoon dried basil
- Salt and pepper to taste
- Fresh parsley for garnish

DIRECTIONS:

1. In a large skillet, heat olive oil over medium heat. Add diced onion and minced garlic, cook until softened.
2. Add ground turkey to the skillet and cook until browned.
3. Stir in diced carrots, diced celery, diced bell pepper, and diced zucchini. Cook until vegetables are tender.
4. Add diced tomatoes (with their juices), dried oregano, dried basil, salt, and pepper. Stir well to combine.
5. Simmer for 10-15 minutes until flavors are blended.
6. Adjust seasoning if necessary.
7. Serve hot, garnished with fresh parsley.

🍽 NUTRITIONAL INFORMATION (PER SERVING):

Calories: 320	
Protein: 25g	
Carbohydrates: 15g	
Fat: 18g	
Fiber: 5g	

10. Cauliflower Rice Stir-Fry with Tofu

INGREDIENTS:

- 1 block (14 oz) firm tofu, cubed
- 1 head cauliflower, riced
- 2 cups mixed vegetables (such as bell peppers, snap peas, and carrots)
- 2 tablespoons sesame oil
- 2 tablespoons soy sauce
- 1 tablespoon rice vinegar
- 1 tablespoon honey
- 1 teaspoon grated ginger
- 2 cloves garlic, minced
- Sesame seeds for garnish

DIRECTIONS:

1. In a large skillet, heat sesame oil over medium heat. Add cubed tofu and cook until golden brown on all sides.
2. Remove tofu from the skillet and set aside.
3. In the same skillet, add riced cauliflower and mixed vegetables. Cook until vegetables are tender-crisp.
4. In a small bowl, whisk together soy sauce, rice vinegar, honey, grated ginger, and minced garlic to make the sauce.
5. Add cooked tofu back to the skillet and pour the sauce over the tofu and vegetables. Stir well to coat.
6. Cook for another minute until everything is heated through.
7. Garnish with sesame seeds before serving.

🍽 NUTRITIONAL INFORMATION (PER SERVING):

Calories: 280	
Protein: 18g	
Carbohydrates: 20g	
Fat: 15g	
Fiber: 8g	

11. Spaghetti Squash with Turkey Bolognese

INGREDIENTS:

- 1 large spaghetti squash
- 1 lb ground turkey
- 1 onion, diced
- 2 cloves garlic, minced
- 1 can (14 oz) crushed tomatoes
- 1 teaspoon dried basil
- 1 teaspoon dried oregano
- Salt and pepper to taste
- Fresh parsley for garnish

DIRECTIONS:

1. Preheat the oven to 375°F (190°C).
2. Cut the spaghetti squash in half lengthwise and scoop out the seeds.
3. Place the squash halves, cut side down, on a baking sheet lined with parchment paper.
4. Bake for 35-45 minutes until the squash is tender and easily pierced with a fork.
5. Meanwhile, in a large skillet, cook ground turkey over medium heat until browned.
6. Add diced onion and minced garlic to the skillet. Cook until softened.
7. Stir in crushed tomatoes, dried basil, dried oregano, salt, and pepper. Simmer for 10-15 minutes.
8. Use a fork to scrape the cooked spaghetti squash strands into a bowl.
9. Serve the turkey bolognese sauce over the spaghetti squash.
10. Garnish with fresh parsley before serving.

NUTRITIONAL INFORMATION (PER SERVING):

Calories: 320	
Protein: 25g	
Carbohydrates: 30g	
Fat: 12g	
Fiber: 8g	

12. Lemon Garlic Shrimp Zoodles

INGREDIENTS:

- 1 lb shrimp, peeled and deveined
- 4 medium zucchinis, spiralized into zoodles
- 2 tablespoons olive oil
- 4 cloves garlic, minced
- 1 teaspoon lemon zest
- 2 tablespoons lemon juice
- Salt and pepper to taste
- Fresh parsley for garnish

DIRECTIONS:

1. Heat olive oil in a large skillet over medium-high heat. Add minced garlic and cook until fragrant.
2. Add shrimp to the skillet and cook until pink and opaque.
3. Add spiralized zucchini noodles to the skillet.
4. Stir in lemon zest, lemon juice, salt, and pepper. Cook for 2-3 minutes until zoodles are tender.
5. Adjust seasoning if necessary.
6. Garnish with fresh parsley before serving.

NUTRITIONAL INFORMATION (PER SERVING):

Calories: 280	
Protein: 30g	
Carbohydrates: 10g	
Fat: 14g	
Fiber: 3g	

13. Chicken and Vegetable Curry

INGREDIENTS:

- 1 lb boneless, skinless chicken breasts, cut into bite-sized pieces
- 2 tablespoons olive oil
- 1 onion, diced
- 2 cloves garlic, minced
- 1 tablespoon grated ginger
- 2 carrots, diced
- 1 bell pepper, diced
- 1 zucchini, diced
- 1 can (14 oz) coconut milk
- 2 tablespoons curry powder
- Salt and pepper to taste
- Fresh cilantro for garnish

DIRECTIONS:

1. In a large skillet, heat olive oil over medium heat. Add diced onion, minced garlic, and grated ginger. Cook until onion is softened.
2. Add chicken pieces to the skillet and cook until browned.
3. Stir in diced carrots, diced bell pepper, and diced zucchini. Cook until vegetables are tender.
4. Pour coconut milk into the skillet and stir in curry powder, salt, and pepper.
5. Simmer for 10-15 minutes until chicken is cooked through and flavors are blended.
6. Adjust seasoning if necessary.
7. Serve hot, garnished with fresh cilantro.

NUTRITIONAL INFORMATION (PER SERVING):

Calories: 320	
Protein: 25g	
Carbohydrates: 15g	
Fat: 18g	
Fiber: 5g	

14. Mediterranean Baked Cod

INGREDIENTS:

- 4 cod fillets (6 oz each)
- 2 tablespoons olive oil
- 2 cloves garlic, minced
- 1 teaspoon dried oregano
- 1 teaspoon dried basil
- 1/2 teaspoon smoked paprika
- Salt and pepper to taste
- 1 lemon, sliced
- Fresh parsley for garnish

DIRECTIONS:

1. Preheat the oven to 400°F (200°C).
2. Place cod fillets in a baking dish.
3. In a small bowl, mix olive oil, minced garlic, dried oregano, dried basil, smoked paprika, salt, and pepper.
4. Brush the olive oil mixture over the cod fillets.
5. Top each fillet with lemon slices.
6. Bake for 15-20 minutes until the fish flakes easily with a fork.
7. Garnish with fresh parsley before serving.

NUTRITIONAL INFORMATION (PER SERVING):

Calories: 280	
Protein: 30g	
Carbohydrates: 2g	
Fat: 16g	
Fiber: 0g	

15. Vegan Lentil Shepherd's Pie

INGREDIENTS:

- 1 cup dried green lentils
- 4 cups vegetable broth
- 2 tablespoons olive oil
- 1 onion, diced
- 2 carrots, diced
- 2 celery stalks, diced
- 2 cloves garlic, minced
- 1 teaspoon dried thyme
- 1 teaspoon dried rosemary
- Salt and pepper to taste
- 4 cups mashed potatoes (prepared)
- Fresh parsley for garnish

DIRECTIONS:

1. In a large pot, combine dried lentils and vegetable broth. Bring to a boil, then reduce heat and simmer for 20-25 minutes until lentils are tender.
2. In a skillet, heat olive oil over medium heat. Add diced onion, diced carrots, diced celery, and minced garlic. Cook until vegetables are softened.
3. Stir cooked lentils, dried thyme, dried rosemary, salt, and pepper into the skillet.
4. Preheat the oven to 375°F (190°C).
5. Transfer the lentil mixture to a baking dish.
6. Spread mashed potatoes over the lentil mixture.
7. Bake for 20-25 minutes until the top is golden brown.
8. Garnish with fresh parsley before serving.

🍲 NUTRITIONAL INFORMATION (PER SERVING):

Calories: 320	
Protein: 15g	
Carbohydrates: 45g	
Fat: 10g	
Fiber: 12g	

16. Thai Coconut Curry Tofu

INGREDIENTS:

- 1 block (14 oz) firm tofu, cubed
- 2 tablespoons olive oil
- 1 onion, diced
- 2 cloves garlic, minced
- 1 tablespoon grated ginger
- 1 red bell pepper, sliced
- 1 yellow bell pepper, sliced
- 1 can (14 oz) coconut milk
- 2 tablespoons red curry paste
- 1 tablespoon soy sauce
- 1 tablespoon maple syrup
- Salt and pepper to taste
- Fresh cilantro for garnish

DIRECTIONS:

1. In a large skillet, heat olive oil over medium heat. Add cubed tofu and cook until golden brown on all sides. Remove tofu from the skillet and set aside.
2. In the same skillet, add diced onion, minced garlic, and grated ginger. Cook until softened.
3. Add sliced red bell pepper and sliced yellow bell pepper to the skillet. Cook until peppers are tender-crisp.
4. Stir in coconut milk, red curry paste, soy sauce, maple syrup, salt, and pepper. Simmer for 5-7 minutes.
5. Add cooked tofu back to the skillet and simmer for another 2-3 minutes.
6. Adjust seasoning if necessary.
7. Serve hot, garnished with fresh cilantro.

🍲 NUTRITIONAL INFORMATION (PER SERVING):

Calories: 320	
Protein: 15g	
Carbohydrates: 20g	
Fat: 25g	
Fiber: 5g	

CHAPTER 7

SALAT RECIPES

1. Kale and Quinoa Salad

INGREDIENTS:

- 4 cups chopped kale
- 1 cup cooked quinoa
- 1/2 cup cherry tomatoes, halved
- 1/4 cup sliced almonds
- 1/4 cup dried cranberries
- 2 tablespoons olive oil
- 1 tablespoon lemon juice
- 1 teaspoon Dijon mustard
- Salt and pepper to taste

DIRECTIONS:

1. In a large bowl, combine chopped kale, cooked quinoa, cherry tomatoes, sliced almonds, and dried cranberries.
2. In a small bowl, whisk together olive oil, lemon juice, Dijon mustard, salt, and pepper to make the dressing.
3. Pour the dressing over the salad and toss to coat evenly.
4. Serve immediately or refrigerate for later.

2. Arugula and Beet Salad

INGREDIENTS:

- 4 cups arugula
- 2 medium beets, roasted and sliced
- 1/4 cup crumbled feta cheese
- 1/4 cup walnuts, chopped
- 2 tablespoons balsamic vinegar
- 1 tablespoon olive oil
- 1 teaspoon honey
- Salt and pepper to taste

DIRECTIONS:

1. In a large bowl, combine arugula, roasted beet slices, crumbled feta cheese, and chopped walnuts.
2. In a small bowl, whisk together balsamic vinegar, olive oil, honey, salt, and pepper to make the dressing.
3. Pour the dressing over the salad and toss to coat evenly.
4. Serve immediately.

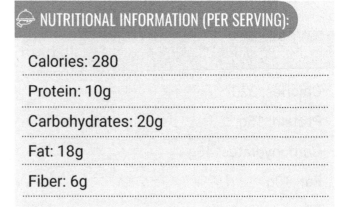

NUTRITIONAL INFORMATION (PER SERVING):

Calories:	280
Protein:	10g
Carbohydrates:	30g
Fat:	14g
Fiber:	6g

NUTRITIONAL INFORMATION (PER SERVING):

Calories:	280
Protein:	10g
Carbohydrates:	20g
Fat:	18g
Fiber:	6g

3. Spinach and Strawberry Salad

INGREDIENTS:

- 4 cups baby spinach
- 1 cup sliced strawberries
- 1/4 cup sliced almonds
- 1/4 cup crumbled goat cheese
- 2 tablespoons balsamic vinegar
- 1 tablespoon olive oil
- 1 teaspoon honey
- Salt and pepper to taste

DIRECTIONS:

1. In a large bowl, combine baby spinach, sliced strawberries, sliced almonds, and crumbled goat cheese.
2. In a small bowl, whisk together balsamic vinegar, olive oil, honey, salt, and pepper to make the dressing.
3. Pour the dressing over the salad and toss to coat evenly.
4. Serve immediately.

NUTRITIONAL INFORMATION (PER SERVING):

Calories: 240

Protein: 8g

Carbohydrates: 15g

Fat: 16g

Fiber: 6g

4. Mediterranean Chickpea Salad

INGREDIENTS:

- 2 cups cooked chickpeas
- 1 cucumber, diced
- 1 bell pepper, diced
- 1/2 cup cherry tomatoes, halved
- 1/4 cup diced red onion
- 1/4 cup chopped fresh parsley
- 2 tablespoons lemon juice
- 2 tablespoons olive oil
- 1 teaspoon dried oregano
- Salt and pepper to taste

DIRECTIONS:

1. In a large bowl, combine cooked chickpeas, diced cucumber, diced bell pepper, cherry tomatoes, diced red onion, and chopped fresh parsley.
2. In a small bowl, whisk together lemon juice, olive oil, dried oregano, salt, and pepper to make the dressing.
3. Pour the dressing over the salad and toss to coat evenly.
4. Serve immediately or refrigerate for later.

NUTRITIONAL INFORMATION (PER SERVING):

Calories: 280

Protein: 10g

Carbohydrates: 35g

Fat: 12g

Fiber: 10g

5. Avocado and Black Bean Salad

INGREDIENTS:

- 2 avocados, diced
- 1 can (15 oz) black beans, drained and rinsed
- 1 bell pepper, diced
- 1/4 cup diced red onion
- 1/4 cup chopped fresh cilantro
- 2 tablespoons lime juice
- 2 tablespoons olive oil
- 1 teaspoon ground cumin
- Salt and pepper to taste

DIRECTIONS:

1. In a large bowl, combine diced avocados, black beans, diced bell pepper, diced red onion, and chopped fresh cilantro.
2. In a small bowl, whisk together lime juice, olive oil, ground cumin, salt, and pepper to make the dressing.
3. Pour the dressing over the salad and toss to coat evenly.
4. Serve immediately or refrigerate for later.

🍽 NUTRITIONAL INFORMATION (PER SERVING):

Calories: 320	
Protein: 10g	
Carbohydrates: 25g	
Fat: 20g	
Fiber: 10g	

6. Quinoa and Kale Salad with Lemon Vinaigrette

INGREDIENTS:

- 2 cups cooked quinoa
- 4 cups chopped kale
- 1/4 cup dried cranberries
- 1/4 cup sliced almonds
- 1/4 cup crumbled feta cheese
- 2 tablespoons lemon juice
- 2 tablespoons olive oil
- 1 teaspoon honey
- Salt and pepper to taste

DIRECTIONS:

1. In a large bowl, combine cooked quinoa, chopped kale, dried cranberries, sliced almonds, and crumbled feta cheese.
2. In a small bowl, whisk together lemon juice, olive oil, honey, salt, and pepper to make the dressing.
3. Pour the dressing over the salad and toss to coat evenly.
4. Serve immediately or refrigerate for later.

🍽 NUTRITIONAL INFORMATION (PER SERVING):

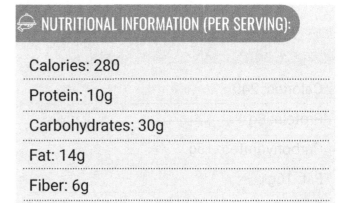

Calories: 280	
Protein: 10g	
Carbohydrates: 30g	
Fat: 14g	
Fiber: 6g	

7. Beet and Goat Cheese Salad

INGREDIENTS:

- 4 cups mixed greens
- 2 medium beets, roasted and sliced
- 1/4 cup crumbled goat cheese
- 1/4 cup chopped walnuts
- 2 tablespoons balsamic vinegar
- 2 tablespoons olive oil
- 1 teaspoon honey
- Salt and pepper to taste

DIRECTIONS:

1. In a large bowl, combine mixed greens, roasted beet slices, crumbled goat cheese, and chopped walnuts.
2. In a small bowl, whisk together balsamic vinegar, olive oil, honey, salt, and pepper to make the dressing.
3. Pour the dressing over the salad and toss to coat evenly.
4. Serve immediately.

⌂ NUTRITIONAL INFORMATION (PER SERVING):

Calories: 280

Protein: 8g

Carbohydrates: 20g

Fat: 18g

Fiber: 6g

8. Spinach and Quinoa Salad with Citrus Vinaigrette

INGREDIENTS:

- 4 cups baby spinach
- 1 cup cooked quinoa
- 1 orange, peeled and segmented
- 1/4 cup sliced almonds
- 2 tablespoons orange juice
- 2 tablespoons olive oil
- 1 teaspoon Dijon mustard
- Salt and pepper to taste

DIRECTIONS:

1. In a large bowl, combine baby spinach, cooked quinoa, orange segments, and sliced almonds.
2. In a small bowl, whisk together orange juice, olive oil, Dijon mustard, salt, and pepper to make the dressing.
3. Pour the dressing over the salad and toss to coat evenly.
4. Serve immediately or refrigerate for later.

⌂ NUTRITIONAL INFORMATION (PER SERVING):

Calories: 280

Protein: 10g

Carbohydrates: 30g

Fat: 14g

Fiber: 6g

9. Tomato and Mozzarella Salad

INGREDIENTS:

- 2 cups cherry tomatoes, halved
- 1 cup fresh mozzarella balls, halved
- 1/4 cup chopped fresh basil
- 2 tablespoons balsamic vinegar
- 2 tablespoons olive oil
- Salt and pepper to taste

DIRECTIONS:

1. In a large bowl, combine cherry tomatoes, fresh mozzarella balls, and chopped fresh basil.
2. In a small bowl, whisk together balsamic vinegar, olive oil, salt, and pepper to make the dressing.
3. Pour the dressing over the salad and toss to coat evenly.
4. Serve immediately.

🛎 NUTRITIONAL INFORMATION (PER SERVING):

Calories: 280	
Protein: 10g	
Carbohydrates: 10g	
Fat: 20g	
Fiber: 2g	

10. Mediterranean Cucumber Salad

INGREDIENTS:

- 2 cucumbers, thinly sliced
- 1 cup cherry tomatoes, halved
- 1/4 cup sliced red onion
- 1/4 cup chopped fresh parsley
- 2 tablespoons lemon juice
- 2 tablespoons olive oil
- 1 teaspoon dried oregano
- Salt and pepper to taste

DIRECTIONS:

1. In a large bowl, combine thinly sliced cucumbers, cherry tomatoes, sliced red onion, and chopped fresh parsley.
2. In a small bowl, whisk together lemon juice, olive oil, dried oregano, salt, and pepper to make the dressing.
3. Pour the dressing over the salad and toss to coat evenly.
4. Serve immediately.

🛎 NUTRITIONAL INFORMATION (PER SERVING):

Calories: 180	
Protein: 4g	
Carbohydrates: 15g	
Fat: 12g	
Fiber: 4g	

Certainly! Here are more anti-inflammatory salad recipes for you:

11. Broccoli and Blueberry Salad

INGREDIENTS:

- 4 cups broccoli florets
- 1 cup blueberries
- 1/4 cup sliced almonds
- 1/4 cup diced red onion
- 2 tablespoons apple cider vinegar
- 2 tablespoons olive oil
- 1 teaspoon honey
- Salt and pepper to taste

DIRECTIONS:

1. Blanch broccoli florets in boiling water for 2 minutes, then drain and rinse with cold water.
2. In a large bowl, combine blanched broccoli florets, blueberries, sliced almonds, and diced red onion.
3. In a small bowl, whisk together apple cider vinegar, olive oil, honey, salt, and pepper to make the dressing.
4. Pour the dressing over the salad and toss to coat evenly.
5. Serve immediately.

NUTRITIONAL INFORMATION (PER SERVING):

Calories: 220	
Protein: 7g	
Carbohydrates: 20g	
Fat: 14g	
Fiber: 6g	

12. Beet and Walnut Salad

INGREDIENTS:

- 4 cups mixed greens
- 2 medium beets, roasted and sliced
- 1/4 cup chopped walnuts
- 1/4 cup crumbled goat cheese
- 2 tablespoons balsamic vinegar
- 2 tablespoons olive oil
- Salt and pepper to taste

DIRECTIONS:

1. In a large bowl, combine mixed greens, roasted beet slices, chopped walnuts, and crumbled goat cheese.
2. In a small bowl, whisk together balsamic vinegar, olive oil, salt, and pepper to make the dressing.
3. Pour the dressing over the salad and toss to coat evenly.
4. Serve immediately.

NUTRITIONAL INFORMATION (PER SERVING):

Calories: 280	
Protein: 8g	
Carbohydrates: 20g	
Fat: 18g	
Fiber: 6g	

13. Greek Salad

INGREDIENTS:

- 4 cups chopped romaine lettuce
- 1 cucumber, diced
- 1 bell pepper, diced
- 1/2 cup cherry tomatoes, halved
- 1/4 cup sliced red onion
- 1/4 cup crumbled feta cheese
- 2 tablespoons lemon juice
- 2 tablespoons olive oil
- 1 teaspoon dried oregano
- Salt and pepper to taste

DIRECTIONS:

1. In a large bowl, combine chopped romaine lettuce, diced cucumber, diced bell pepper, cherry tomatoes, sliced red onion, and crumbled feta cheese.
2. In a small bowl, whisk together lemon juice, olive oil, dried oregano, salt, and pepper to make the dressing.
3. Pour the dressing over the salad and toss to coat evenly.
4. Serve immediately.

🛎 NUTRITIONAL INFORMATION (PER SERVING):

Calories: 240	
Protein: 8g	
Carbohydrates: 15g	
Fat: 16g	
Fiber: 6g	

14. Spinach and Strawberry Salad with Poppy Seed Dressing

INGREDIENTS:

- 4 cups baby spinach
- 1 cup sliced strawberries
- 1/4 cup sliced almonds
- 1/4 cup crumbled feta cheese
- 2 tablespoons balsamic vinegar
- 2 tablespoons olive oil
- 1 teaspoon honey
- 1 teaspoon poppy seeds
- Salt and pepper to taste

DIRECTIONS:

1. In a large bowl, combine baby spinach, sliced strawberries, sliced almonds, and crumbled feta cheese.
2. In a small bowl, whisk together balsamic vinegar, olive oil, honey, poppy seeds, salt, and pepper to make the dressing.
3. Pour the dressing over the salad and toss to coat evenly.
4. Serve immediately.

🛎 NUTRITIONAL INFORMATION (PER SERVING):

Calories: 280	
Protein: 8g	
Carbohydrates: 20g	
Fat: 18g	
Fiber: 6g	

15. Kale and Apple Salad with Maple Mustard Dressing

INGREDIENTS:

- 4 cups chopped kale
- 1 apple, thinly sliced
- 1/4 cup dried cranberries
- 1/4 cup sliced almonds
- 2 tablespoons apple cider vinegar
- 2 tablespoons olive oil
- 1 tablespoon maple syrup
- 1 teaspoon Dijon mustard
- Salt and pepper to taste

DIRECTIONS:

1. In a large bowl, combine chopped kale, thinly sliced apple, dried cranberries, and sliced almonds.
2. In a small bowl, whisk together apple cider vinegar, olive oil, maple syrup, Dijon mustard, salt, and pepper to make the dressing.
3. Pour the dressing over the salad and toss to coat evenly.
4. Serve immediately.

🍽 NUTRITIONAL INFORMATION (PER SERVING):

Calories: 240

Protein: 6g

Carbohydrates: 25g

Fat: 15g

Fiber: 6g

16. Mediterranean Quinoa Salad

INGREDIENTS:

- 2 cups cooked quinoa
- 1 cucumber, diced
- 1 bell pepper, diced
- 1/2 cup cherry tomatoes, halved
- 1/4 cup diced red onion
- 1/4 cup chopped fresh parsley
- 2 tablespoons lemon juice
- 2 tablespoons olive oil
- 1 teaspoon dried oregano
- Salt and pepper to taste

DIRECTIONS:

1. In a large bowl, combine cooked quinoa, diced cucumber, diced bell pepper, cherry tomatoes, diced red onion, and chopped fresh parsley.
2. In a small bowl, whisk together lemon juice, olive oil, dried oregano, salt, and pepper to make the dressing.
3. Pour the dressing over the salad and toss to coat evenly.
4. Serve immediately or refrigerate for later.

🍽 NUTRITIONAL INFORMATION (PER SERVING):

Calories: 280

Protein: 8g

Carbohydrates: 35g

Fat: 12g

Fiber: 6g

CHAPTER 8

SOUPS RECIPES

1. Lentil Vegetable Soup

INGREDIENTS:

- 1 cup dried green lentils
- 4 cups vegetable broth
- 1 tablespoon olive oil
- 1 onion, diced
- 2 carrots, diced
- 2 celery stalks, diced
- 2 cloves garlic, minced
- 1 can (14 oz) diced tomatoes
- 2 cups chopped spinach
- 1 teaspoon ground cumin
- 1 teaspoon dried thyme
- Salt and pepper to taste

DIRECTIONS:

1. In a large pot, heat olive oil over medium heat. Add diced onion, diced carrots, diced celery, and minced garlic. Cook until softened.
2. Add dried green lentils and vegetable broth to the pot. Bring to a boil, then reduce heat and simmer for 20-25 minutes until lentils are tender.
3. Stir in diced tomatoes, chopped spinach, ground cumin, dried thyme, salt, and pepper. Simmer for an additional 10 minutes.
4. Adjust seasoning if necessary.
5. Serve hot.

🍽 NUTRITIONAL INFORMATION (PER SERVING):

Calories: 220	
Protein: 12g	
Carbohydrates: 35g	
Fat: 4g	
Fiber: 12g	

2. Turmeric Ginger Carrot Soup

INGREDIENTS:

- 1 tablespoon olive oil
- 1 onion, diced
- 2 cloves garlic, minced
- 1 tablespoon grated ginger
- 1 teaspoon ground turmeric
- 4 cups diced carrots
- 4 cups vegetable broth
- Salt and pepper to taste
- Fresh cilantro for garnish

DIRECTIONS:

1. In a large pot, heat olive oil over medium heat. Add diced onion, minced garlic, grated ginger, and ground turmeric. Cook until fragrant.
2. Add diced carrots and vegetable broth to the pot. Bring to a boil, then reduce heat and simmer for 20-25 minutes until carrots are tender.
3. Use an immersion blender to puree the soup until smooth.
4. Season with salt and pepper to taste.
5. Serve hot, garnished with fresh cilantro.

🍽 NUTRITIONAL INFORMATION (PER SERVING):

Calories: 180	
Protein: 4g	
Carbohydrates: 25g	
Fat: 8g	
Fiber: 6g	

3. Butternut Squash Soup

INGREDIENTS:

- 1 tablespoon olive oil
- 1 onion, diced
- 2 cloves garlic, minced
- 1 butternut squash, peeled, seeded, and diced
- 4 cups vegetable broth
- 1 teaspoon ground cinnamon
- 1/2 teaspoon ground nutmeg
- Salt and pepper to taste
- Coconut milk for garnish

DIRECTIONS:

1. In a large pot, heat olive oil over medium heat. Add diced onion and minced garlic. Cook until softened.
2. Add diced butternut squash and vegetable broth to the pot. Bring to a boil, then reduce heat and simmer for 20-25 minutes until squash is tender.
3. Use an immersion blender to puree the soup until smooth.
4. Stir in ground cinnamon and ground nutmeg. Season with salt and pepper to taste.
5. Serve hot, drizzled with coconut milk.

NUTRITIONAL INFORMATION (PER SERVING):

Calories:	200
Protein:	4g
Carbohydrates:	35g
Fat:	6g
Fiber:	8g

4. Tomato Basil Soup

INGREDIENTS:

- 1 tablespoon olive oil
- 1 onion, diced
- 2 cloves garlic, minced
- 2 cans (14 oz each) diced tomatoes
- 4 cups vegetable broth
- 1 teaspoon dried basil
- Salt and pepper to taste
- Fresh basil for garnish

DIRECTIONS:

1. In a large pot, heat olive oil over medium heat. Add diced onion and minced garlic. Cook until softened.
2. Add diced tomatoes and vegetable broth to the pot. Bring to a boil, then reduce heat and simmer for 15-20 minutes.
3. Use an immersion blender to puree the soup until smooth.
4. Stir in dried basil. Season with salt and pepper to taste.
5. Serve hot, garnished with fresh basil.

NUTRITIONAL INFORMATION (PER SERVING):

Calories:	150
Protein:	4g
Carbohydrates:	25g
Fat:	4g
Fiber:	6g

5. Spinach and White Bean Soup

INGREDIENTS:

- 1 tablespoon olive oil
- 1 onion, diced
- 2 cloves garlic, minced
- 4 cups vegetable broth
- 2 cans (15 oz each) white beans, drained and rinsed
- 4 cups chopped spinach
- 1 teaspoon dried thyme
- Salt and pepper to taste
- Lemon wedges for garnish

DIRECTIONS:

1. In a large pot, heat olive oil over medium heat. Add diced onion and minced garlic. Cook until softened.
2. Add vegetable broth and white beans to the pot. Bring to a boil, then reduce heat and simmer for 10 minutes.
3. Use an immersion blender to partially puree the soup, leaving some beans whole.
4. Stir in chopped spinach and dried thyme. Simmer for an additional 5 minutes until spinach is wilted.
5. Season with salt and pepper to taste.
6. Serve hot, with lemon wedges for garnish.

🍽 NUTRITIONAL INFORMATION (PER SERVING):

Calories: 220

Protein: 10g

Carbohydrates: 35g

Fat: 4g

Fiber: 12g

6. Cauliflower and Leek Soup

INGREDIENTS:

- 1 tablespoon olive oil
- 2 leeks, white and light green parts only, sliced
- 1 head cauliflower, chopped
- 4 cups vegetable broth
- 1 teaspoon dried thyme
- Salt and pepper to taste
- Fresh parsley for garnish

DIRECTIONS:

1. In a large pot, heat olive oil over medium heat. Add sliced leeks and cook until softened.
2. Add chopped cauliflower and vegetable broth to the pot. Bring to a boil, then reduce heat and simmer for 20-25 minutes until cauliflower is tender.
3. Use an immersion blender to puree the soup until smooth.
4. Stir in dried thyme. Season with salt and pepper to taste.
5. Serve hot, garnished with fresh parsley.

🍽 NUTRITIONAL INFORMATION (PER SERVING):

Calories: 160

Protein: 6g

Carbohydrates: 25g

Fat: 6g

Fiber: 8g

7. Spicy Black Bean Soup

INGREDIENTS:

- 1 tablespoon olive oil
- 1 onion, diced
- 2 cloves garlic, minced
- 2 cans (15 oz each) black beans, drained and rinsed
- 4 cups vegetable broth
- 1 teaspoon ground cumin
- 1/2 teaspoon chili powder
- Salt and pepper to taste
- Fresh cilantro for garnish

DIRECTIONS:

1. In a large pot, heat olive oil over medium heat. Add diced onion and minced garlic. Cook until softened.
2. Add black beans and vegetable broth to the pot. Bring to a boil, then reduce heat and simmer for 10 minutes.
3. Use an immersion blender to partially puree the soup, leaving some beans whole.
4. Stir in ground cumin, chili powder, salt, and pepper. Simmer for an additional 5 minutes.
5. Serve hot, garnished with fresh cilantro.

🍲 NUTRITIONAL INFORMATION (PER SERVING):

Calories:	200
Protein:	10g
Carbohydrates:	30g
Fat:	4g
Fiber:	12g

8. Roasted Red Pepper Soup

INGREDIENTS:

- 3 red bell peppers
- 1 tablespoon olive oil
- 1 onion, diced
- 2 cloves garlic, minced
- 4 cups vegetable broth
- 1/2 cup canned coconut milk
- Salt and pepper to taste
- Fresh basil for garnish

DIRECTIONS:

1. Preheat the broiler. Place red bell peppers on a baking sheet and broil until charred on all sides, turning occasionally. Remove from the oven, let cool slightly, then peel, seed, and chop the peppers.
2. In a large pot, heat olive oil over medium heat. Add diced onion and minced garlic. Cook until softened.
3. Add chopped roasted red peppers and vegetable broth to the pot. Bring to a boil, then reduce heat and simmer for 15-20 minutes.
4. Use an immersion blender to puree the soup until smooth.
5. Stir in canned coconut milk. Season with salt and pepper to taste.
6. Serve hot, garnished with fresh basil.

🍲 NUTRITIONAL INFORMATION (PER SERVING):

Calories:	220
Protein:	4g
Carbohydrates:	20g
Fat:	14g
Fiber:	6g

9. Mushroom Barley Soup

INGREDIENTS:

- 1 tablespoon olive oil
- 1 onion, diced
- 2 cloves garlic, minced
- 8 oz mushrooms, sliced
- 1/2 cup pearled barley
- 4 cups vegetable broth
- 1 teaspoon dried thyme
- Salt and pepper to taste
- Fresh parsley for garnish

DIRECTIONS:

1. In a large pot, heat olive oil over medium heat. Add diced onion and minced garlic. Cook until softened.
2. Add sliced mushrooms to the pot. Cook until mushrooms are browned.
3. Stir in pearled barley and vegetable broth. Bring to a boil, then reduce heat and simmer for 30-35 minutes until barley is tender.
4. Stir in dried thyme. Season with salt and pepper to taste.
5. Serve hot, garnished with fresh parsley.

NUTRITIONAL INFORMATION (PER SERVING):

Calories: 220	
Protein: 6g	
Carbohydrates: 35g	
Fat: 4g	
Fiber: 8g	

10. Spinach and Lentil Soup

INGREDIENTS:

- 1 tablespoon olive oil
- 1 onion, diced
- 2 cloves garlic, minced
- 1 cup dried green lentils
- 4 cups vegetable broth
- 4 cups chopped spinach
- 1 teaspoon ground cumin
- Salt and pepper to taste
- Lemon wedges for garnish

DIRECTIONS:

1. In a large pot, heat olive oil over medium heat. Add diced onion and minced garlic. Cook until softened.
2. Add dried green lentils and vegetable broth to the pot. Bring to a boil, then reduce heat and simmer for 20-25 minutes until lentils are tender.
3. Stir in chopped spinach and ground cumin. Simmer for an additional 5 minutes until spinach is wilted.
4. Season with salt and pepper to taste.
5. Serve hot, with lemon wedges for garnish.

NUTRITIONAL INFORMATION (PER SERVING):

Calories: 220	
Protein: 12g	
Carbohydrates: 30g	
Fat: 4g	
Fiber: 12g	

11. Coconut Curry Lentil Soup

INGREDIENTS:

- 1 tablespoon olive oil
- 1 onion, diced
- 2 cloves garlic, minced
- 1 tablespoon grated ginger
- 1 tablespoon curry powder
- 1 cup dried red lentils
- 1 can (14 oz) coconut milk
- 4 cups vegetable broth
- Salt and pepper to taste
- Fresh cilantro for garnish

DIRECTIONS:

1. In a large pot, heat olive oil over medium heat. Add diced onion, minced garlic, and grated ginger. Cook until softened.
2. Stir in curry powder and dried red lentils. Cook for 1-2 minutes.
3. Add coconut milk and vegetable broth to the pot. Bring to a boil, then reduce heat and simmer for 20-25 minutes until lentils are tender.
4. Season with salt and pepper to taste.
5. Serve hot, garnished with fresh cilantro.

🍽 NUTRITIONAL INFORMATION (PER SERVING):

Calories: 280	
Protein: 10g	
Carbohydrates: 30g	
Fat: 14g	
Fiber: 10g	

12. Sweet Potato and Kale Soup

INGREDIENTS:

- 1 tablespoon olive oil
- 1 onion, diced
- 2 cloves garlic, minced
- 2 sweet potatoes, peeled and diced
- 4 cups vegetable broth
- 4 cups chopped kale
- 1/2 teaspoon smoked paprika
- Salt and pepper to taste
- Coconut cream for garnish

DIRECTIONS:

1. In a large pot, heat olive oil over medium heat. Add diced onion and minced garlic. Cook until softened.
2. Add diced sweet potatoes and vegetable broth to the pot. Bring to a boil, then reduce heat and simmer for 20-25 minutes until sweet potatoes are tender.
3. Stir in chopped kale and smoked paprika. Simmer for an additional 5 minutes until kale is wilted.
4. Season with salt and pepper to taste.
5. Serve hot, with a dollop of coconut cream for garnish.

🍽 NUTRITIONAL INFORMATION (PER SERVING):

Calories: 240	
Protein: 6g	
Carbohydrates: 35g	
Fat: 8g	
Fiber: 8g	

13. Cauliflower and Turmeric Soup

INGREDIENTS:

- 1 tablespoon olive oil
- 1 onion, diced
- 2 cloves garlic, minced
- 1 head cauliflower, chopped
- 4 cups vegetable broth
- 1 teaspoon ground turmeric
- 1/2 teaspoon ground cumin
- Salt and pepper to taste
- Fresh parsley for garnish

DIRECTIONS:

1. In a large pot, heat olive oil over medium heat. Add diced onion and minced garlic. Cook until softened.
2. Add chopped cauliflower and vegetable broth to the pot. Bring to a boil, then reduce heat and simmer for 20-25 minutes until cauliflower is tender.
3. Use an immersion blender to puree the soup until smooth.
4. Stir in ground turmeric, ground cumin, salt, and pepper. Simmer for an additional 5 minutes.
5. Serve hot, garnished with fresh parsley.

🍽 NUTRITIONAL INFORMATION (PER SERVING):

Calories: 180

Protein: 6g

Carbohydrates: 25g

Fat: 6g

Fiber: 8g

14. Quinoa Vegetable Soup

INGREDIENTS:

- 1 tablespoon olive oil
- 1 onion, diced
- 2 cloves garlic, minced
- 2 carrots, diced
- 2 celery stalks, diced
- 1 zucchini, diced
- 1/2 cup quinoa
- 4 cups vegetable broth
- 1 teaspoon dried thyme
- Salt and pepper to taste
- Fresh parsley for garnish

DIRECTIONS:

1. In a large pot, heat olive oil over medium heat. Add diced onion and minced garlic. Cook until softened.
2. Add diced carrots, diced celery, diced zucchini, and quinoa to the pot. Cook for 1-2 minutes.
3. Add vegetable broth to the pot. Bring to a boil, then reduce heat and simmer for 15-20 minutes until vegetables are tender and quinoa is cooked.
4. Stir in dried thyme. Season with salt and pepper to taste.
5. Serve hot, garnished with fresh parsley.

🍽 NUTRITIONAL INFORMATION (PER SERVING):

Calories: 220

Protein: 8g

Carbohydrates: 30g

Fat: 6g

Fiber: 8g

15. Ginger Carrot and Coconut Soup

INGREDIENTS:

- 1 tablespoon olive oil
- 1 onion, diced
- 2 cloves garlic, minced
- 1 tablespoon grated ginger
- 6 carrots, peeled and chopped
- 4 cups vegetable broth
- 1 can (14 oz) coconut milk
- Salt and pepper to taste
- Fresh cilantro for garnish

DIRECTIONS:

1. In a large pot, heat olive oil over medium heat. Add diced onion, minced garlic, and grated ginger. Cook until softened.
2. Add chopped carrots and vegetable broth to the pot. Bring to a boil, then reduce heat and simmer for 20-25 minutes until carrots are tender.
3. Use an immersion blender to puree the soup until smooth.
4. Stir in coconut milk. Season with salt and pepper to taste.
5. Serve hot, garnished with fresh cilantro.

🍽 NUTRITIONAL INFORMATION (PER SERVING):

Calories: 240

Protein: 4g

Carbohydrates: 20g

Fat: 18g

Fiber: 6g

16. Broccoli and Kale Soup

INGREDIENTS:

- 1 tablespoon olive oil
- 1 onion, diced
- 2 cloves garlic, minced
- 1 head broccoli, chopped
- 4 cups chopped kale
- 4 cups vegetable broth
- 1/4 teaspoon red pepper flakes
- Salt and pepper to taste
- Lemon wedges for garnish

DIRECTIONS:

1. In a large pot, heat olive oil over medium heat. Add diced onion and minced garlic. Cook until softened.
2. Add chopped broccoli, chopped kale, and vegetable broth to the pot. Bring to a boil, then reduce heat and simmer for 15-20 minutes until vegetables are tender.
3. Use an immersion blender to partially puree the soup, leaving some chunks of vegetables.
4. Stir in red pepper flakes. Season with salt and pepper to taste.
5. Serve hot, with lemon wedges for garnish.

🍽 NUTRITIONAL INFORMATION (PER SERVING):

Calories: 180

Protein: 8g

Carbohydrates: 25g

Fat: 6g

Fiber: 10g

CHAPTER 9

PASTA RECIPES

1. Tomato Basil Pasta

INGREDIENTS:

- 8 oz whole wheat pasta
- 2 tablespoons olive oil
- 3 cloves garlic, minced
- 2 cups cherry tomatoes, halved
- 1/4 cup chopped fresh basil
- Salt and pepper to taste
- Grated Parmesan cheese for serving (optional)

DIRECTIONS:

1. Cook the whole wheat pasta according to package instructions until al dente. Drain and set aside.
2. In a large skillet, heat olive oil over medium heat. Add minced garlic and cook until fragrant, about 1 minute.
3. Add cherry tomatoes to the skillet and cook until they start to soften, about 5 minutes.
4. Stir in the cooked pasta and chopped fresh basil. Season with salt and pepper to taste.
5. Serve hot, optionally topped with grated Parmesan cheese.

NUTRITIONAL INFORMATION (PER SERVING):

Calories:	350
Protein:	10g
Carbohydrates:	50g
Fat:	12g
Fiber:	8g

2. Lemon Garlic Shrimp Pasta

INGREDIENTS:

- 8 oz whole grain spaghetti
- 1 tablespoon olive oil
- 3 cloves garlic, minced
- 1 pound shrimp, peeled and deveined
- Zest of 1 lemon
- Juice of 1 lemon
- Salt and pepper to taste
- Chopped parsley for garnish

DIRECTIONS:

1. Cook the whole grain spaghetti according to package instructions until al dente. Drain and set aside.
2. In a large skillet, heat olive oil over medium heat. Add minced garlic and cook until fragrant, about 1 minute.
3. Add shrimp to the skillet and cook until they turn pink and opaque, about 3-4 minutes.
4. Stir in the cooked pasta, lemon zest, and lemon juice. Season with salt and pepper to taste.
5. Serve hot, garnished with chopped parsley.

NUTRITIONAL INFORMATION (PER SERVING):

Calories:	380
Protein:	30g
Carbohydrates:	40g
Fat:	10g
Fiber:	6g

3. Spinach Mushroom Pasta

INGREDIENTS:

- 8 oz whole wheat penne
- 2 tablespoons olive oil
- 3 cloves garlic, minced
- 8 oz mushrooms, sliced
- 4 cups fresh spinach
- Salt and pepper to taste
- Red pepper flakes for heat (optional)

DIRECTIONS:

1. Cook the whole wheat penne according to package instructions until al dente. Drain and set aside.
2. In a large skillet, heat olive oil over medium heat. Add minced garlic and cook until fragrant, about 1 minute.
3. Add sliced mushrooms to the skillet and cook until they release their juices and become tender, about 5 minutes.
4. Stir in fresh spinach and cook until wilted, about 2 minutes.
5. Add the cooked pasta to the skillet and toss to combine. Season with salt, pepper, and red pepper flakes if using.
6. Serve hot.

NUTRITIONAL INFORMATION (PER SERVING):

Calories: 320
....
Protein: 12g
....
Carbohydrates: 50g
....
Fat: 8g
....
Fiber: 8g

4. Roasted Vegetable Pasta

INGREDIENTS:

- 8 oz whole grain fusilli
- 2 tablespoons olive oil
- 2 bell peppers, sliced
- 1 zucchini, sliced
- 1 yellow squash, sliced
- 1 red onion, sliced
- 3 cloves garlic, minced
- 1 teaspoon dried oregano
- Salt and pepper to taste

DIRECTIONS:

1. Preheat the oven to 400°F (200°C). Line a baking sheet with parchment paper.
2. In a large bowl, toss sliced bell peppers, zucchini, yellow squash, and red onion with olive oil, minced garlic, dried oregano, salt, and pepper until evenly coated.
3. Spread the vegetables in a single layer on the prepared baking sheet. Roast in the preheated oven for 20-25 minutes, or until tender and slightly caramelized.
4. Cook the whole grain fusilli according to package instructions until al dente. Drain and set aside.
5. Toss the roasted vegetables with the cooked pasta.
6. Serve hot.

NUTRITIONAL INFORMATION (PER SERVING):

Calories: 360
....
Protein: 10g
....
Carbohydrates: 60g
....
Fat: 10g
....
Fiber: 12g

5. Avocado Pesto Pasta

INGREDIENTS:

- 8 oz whole wheat spaghetti
- 1 ripe avocado
- 1 cup fresh basil leaves
- 2 cloves garlic
- 2 tablespoons lemon juice
- 1/4 cup olive oil
- Salt and pepper to taste
- Cherry tomatoes for garnish

DIRECTIONS:

1. Cook the whole wheat spaghetti according to package instructions until al dente. Drain and set aside.
2. In a food processor, combine ripe avocado, fresh basil leaves, minced garlic, lemon juice, olive oil, salt, and pepper. Blend until smooth.
3. Toss the cooked pasta with the avocado pesto sauce until evenly coated.
4. Serve hot, garnished with cherry tomatoes.

NUTRITIONAL INFORMATION (PER SERVING):

Calories: 380

Protein: 8g

Carbohydrates: 50g

Fat: 18g

Fiber: 10g

6. Mediterranean Chickpea Pasta

INGREDIENTS:

- 8 oz whole grain penne
- 1 tablespoon olive oil
- 3 cloves garlic, minced
- 1 can (15 oz) chickpeas, drained and rinsed
- 1 cup cherry tomatoes, halved
- 1/4 cup chopped Kalamata olives
- 2 tablespoons chopped fresh parsley
- Salt and pepper to taste

DIRECTIONS:

1. Cook the whole grain penne according to package instructions until al dente. Drain and set aside.
2. In a large skillet, heat olive oil over medium heat. Add minced garlic and cook until fragrant, about 1 minute.
3. Add chickpeas to the skillet and cook for 3-4 minutes.
4. Stir in cherry tomatoes and chopped Kalamata olives. Cook for an additional 2 minutes.
5. Add the cooked pasta to the skillet and toss to combine. Season with salt and pepper to taste.
6. Serve hot, garnished with chopped fresh parsley.

NUTRITIONAL INFORMATION (PER SERVING):

Calories: 380

Protein: 14g

Carbohydrates: 60g

Fat: 10g

Fiber: 12g

7. Spaghetti with Garlic and Broccoli

INGREDIENTS:

- 8 oz whole wheat spaghetti
- 2 tablespoons olive oil
- 4 cloves garlic, minced
- 2 cups broccoli florets
- Zest of 1 lemon
- Salt and pepper to taste
- Grated Parmesan cheese for serving (optional)

DIRECTIONS:

1. Cook the whole wheat spaghetti according to package instructions until al dente. Drain and set aside.
2. In a large skillet, heat olive oil over medium heat. Add minced garlic and cook until fragrant, about 1 minute.
3. Add broccoli florets to the skillet and cook until tender, about 5 minutes.
4. Stir in cooked spaghetti and lemon zest. Season with salt and pepper to taste.
5. Serve hot, optionally topped with grated Parmesan cheese.

NUTRITIONAL INFORMATION (PER SERVING):

Calories:	320
Protein:	10g
Carbohydrates:	50g
Fat:	10g
Fiber:	8g

8. Zucchini Noodles with Marinara Sauce

INGREDIENTS:

- 4 medium zucchini
- 1 tablespoon olive oil
- 2 cloves garlic, minced
- 1 can (14 oz) crushed tomatoes
- 1 teaspoon dried oregano
- Salt and pepper to taste
- Fresh basil for garnish

DIRECTIONS:

1. Use a spiralizer to spiralize the zucchini into noodles. Set aside.
2. In a large skillet, heat olive oil over medium heat. Add minced garlic and cook until fragrant, about 1 minute.
3. Add crushed tomatoes and dried oregano to the skillet. Simmer for 5-7 minutes.
4. Add zucchini noodles to the skillet and toss to coat in the marinara sauce. Cook for 2-3 minutes until heated through.
5. Season with salt and pepper to taste.
6. Serve hot, garnished with fresh basil.

NUTRITIONAL INFORMATION (PER SERVING):

Calories:	120
Protein:	4g
Carbohydrates:	20g
Fat:	4g
Fiber:	6g

9. Arugula Walnut Pesto Pasta

INGREDIENTS:

- 8 oz whole grain linguine
- 2 cups packed arugula
- 1/2 cup walnuts
- 2 cloves garlic
- 1/4 cup grated Parmesan cheese
- 1/4 cup olive oil
- Salt and pepper to taste
- Lemon wedges for garnish

DIRECTIONS:

1. Cook the whole grain linguine according to package instructions until al dente. Drain and set aside.
2. In a food processor, combine arugula, walnuts, minced garlic, grated Parmesan cheese, olive oil, salt, and pepper. Blend until smooth.
3. Toss the cooked pasta with the arugula walnut pesto sauce until evenly coated.
4. Serve hot, with lemon wedges for garnish.

NUTRITIONAL INFORMATION (PER SERVING):

Calories: 380

Protein: 10g

Carbohydrates: 45g

Fat: 20g

Fiber: 8g

10. Spinach Artichoke Pasta

INGREDIENTS:

- 8 oz whole wheat penne
- 1 tablespoon olive oil
- 2 cloves garlic, minced
- 1 can (14 oz) artichoke hearts, drained and chopped
- 2 cups fresh spinach
- 1/4 cup grated Parmesan cheese
- Salt and pepper to taste

DIRECTIONS:

1. Cook the whole wheat penne according to package instructions until al dente. Drain and set aside.
2. In a large skillet, heat olive oil over medium heat. Add minced garlic and cook until fragrant, about 1 minute.
3. Add chopped artichoke hearts to the skillet and cook for 2-3 minutes.
4. Stir in fresh spinach and cook until wilted, about 2 minutes.
5. Add the cooked pasta to the skillet and toss to combine. Sprinkle grated Parmesan cheese over the top.
6. Serve hot.

NUTRITIONAL INFORMATION (PER SERVING):

Calories: 320

Protein: 12g

Carbohydrates: 45g

Fat: 8g

Fiber: 8g

11. Eggplant Tomato Pasta

INGREDIENTS:

- 8 oz whole grain spaghetti
- 1 eggplant, diced
- 2 tablespoons olive oil
- 2 cloves garlic, minced
- 1 can (14 oz) diced tomatoes
- 1 teaspoon dried basil
- Salt and pepper to taste
- Fresh basil for garnish

DIRECTIONS:

1. Cook the whole grain spaghetti according to package instructions until al dente. Drain and set aside.
2. In a large skillet, heat olive oil over medium heat. Add diced eggplant and cook until softened and lightly browned, about 5 minutes.
3. Add minced garlic to the skillet and cook until fragrant, about 1 minute.
4. Stir in diced tomatoes and dried basil. Simmer for 5-7 minutes.
5. Add the cooked pasta to the skillet and toss to combine.
6. Season with salt and pepper to taste. Serve hot, garnished with fresh basil.

NUTRITIONAL INFORMATION (PER SERVING):

Calories: 350

Protein: 10g

Carbohydrates: 55g

Fat: 10g

Fiber: 10g

12. Cauliflower Alfredo Pasta

INGREDIENTS:

- 8 oz whole wheat fettuccine
- 1 head cauliflower, chopped
- 2 cloves garlic, minced
- 2 cups vegetable broth
- 1/2 cup unsweetened almond milk
- 1/4 cup nutritional yeast
- Salt and pepper to taste
- Chopped parsley for garnish

DIRECTIONS:

1. Cook the whole wheat fettuccine according to package instructions until al dente. Drain and set aside.
2. In a large pot, combine chopped cauliflower, minced garlic, and vegetable broth. Bring to a boil, then reduce heat and simmer for 10-15 minutes until cauliflower is tender.
3. Use an immersion blender to puree the cauliflower mixture until smooth.
4. Stir in unsweetened almond milk, nutritional yeast, salt, and pepper.
5. Add the cooked pasta to the pot and toss to coat in the cauliflower Alfredo sauce.
6. Serve hot, garnished with chopped parsley.

NUTRITIONAL INFORMATION (PER SERVING):

Calories: 320

Protein: 12g

Carbohydrates: 55g

Fat: 6g

Fiber: 10g

13. Red Lentil Pasta with Roasted Vegetables

INGREDIENTS:

- 8 oz red lentil pasta
- 1 tablespoon olive oil
- 2 cups mixed vegetables (such as bell peppers, zucchini, and cherry tomatoes), chopped
- 2 cloves garlic, minced
- 1 teaspoon dried Italian seasoning
- Salt and pepper to taste

DIRECTIONS:

1. Cook the red lentil pasta according to package instructions until al dente. Drain and set aside.
2. Preheat the oven to 400°F (200°C). Line a baking sheet with parchment paper.
3. In a large bowl, toss chopped mixed vegetables with olive oil, minced garlic, dried Italian seasoning, salt, and pepper until evenly coated.
4. Spread the vegetables in a single layer on the prepared baking sheet. Roast in the preheated oven for 20-25 minutes, or until tender and slightly caramelized.
5. Toss the roasted vegetables with the cooked pasta.
6. Serve hot.

🍽 NUTRITIONAL INFORMATION (PER SERVING):

Calories: 350

Protein: 15g

Carbohydrates: 55g

Fat: 8g

Fiber: 12g

14. Creamy Butternut Squash Pasta

INGREDIENTS:

- 8 oz whole wheat spaghetti
- 2 cups butternut squash, diced
- 2 cloves garlic, minced
- 1 tablespoon olive oil
- 1/2 cup unsweetened almond milk
- 2 tablespoons nutritional yeast
- 1/2 teaspoon dried sage
- Salt and pepper to taste
- Chopped parsley for garnish

DIRECTIONS:

1. Cook the whole wheat spaghetti according to package instructions until al dente. Drain and set aside.
2. In a large pot, heat olive oil over medium heat. Add minced garlic and cook until fragrant, about 1 minute.
3. Add diced butternut squash to the pot and cook until softened, about 10 minutes.
4. Use an immersion blender to puree the butternut squash until smooth.
5. Stir in unsweetened almond milk, nutritional yeast, dried sage, salt, and pepper.
6. Add the cooked pasta to the pot and toss to coat in the creamy butternut squash sauce.
7. Serve hot, garnished with chopped parsley.

🍽 NUTRITIONAL INFORMATION (PER SERVING):

Calories: 340

Protein: 10g

Carbohydrates: 60g

Fat: 8g

Fiber: 12g

15. Mediterranean Pasta Salad

INGREDIENTS:

- 8 oz whole wheat rotini
- 1 cup cherry tomatoes, halved
- 1/2 cup diced cucumber
- 1/4 cup sliced Kalamata olives
- 1/4 cup crumbled feta cheese
- 2 tablespoons chopped fresh parsley
- 2 tablespoons olive oil
- 1 tablespoon red wine vinegar
- 1 teaspoon dried oregano
- Salt and pepper to taste

DIRECTIONS:

1. Cook the whole wheat rotini according to package instructions until al dente. Drain and rinse under cold water to cool.
2. In a large bowl, combine cooked rotini, cherry tomatoes, diced cucumber, sliced Kalamata olives, crumbled feta cheese, and chopped fresh parsley.
3. In a small bowl, whisk together olive oil, red wine vinegar, dried oregano, salt, and pepper.
4. Pour the dressing over the pasta salad and toss to coat evenly.
5. Serve chilled or at room temperature.

⟁ NUTRITIONAL INFORMATION (PER SERVING):

Calories: 320

Protein: 10g

Carbohydrates: 45g

Fat: 12g

Fiber: 18g

16. Pesto Zucchini Noodles with Cherry Tomatoes

INGREDIENTS:

- 4 medium zucchini
- 1 cup cherry tomatoes, halved
- 1/4 cup pine nuts
- 2 cloves garlic
- 1/4 cup grated Parmesan cheese
- 1/4 cup olive oil
- Salt and pepper to taste
- Fresh basil for garnish

DIRECTIONS:

1. Use a spiralizer to spiralize the zucchini into noodles. Set aside.
2. In a food processor, combine cherry tomatoes, pine nuts, minced garlic, grated Parmesan cheese, olive oil, salt, and pepper. Pulse until well combined but still slightly chunky.
3. Toss the zucchini noodles with the pesto sauce until evenly coated.
4. Serve chilled or at room temperature, garnished with fresh basil.

⟁ NUTRITIONAL INFORMATION (PER SERVING):

Calories: 250

Protein: 8g

Carbohydrates: 12g

Fat: 20g

Fiber: 4g

CHAPTER 10

FISH AND SEAFOOD RECIPES

1. Baked Salmon with Lemon and Dill

INGREDIENTS:

- 4 salmon fillets (4-6 oz each)
- 2 tablespoons olive oil
- 2 tablespoons fresh lemon juice
- 2 cloves garlic, minced
- 1 tablespoon chopped fresh dill
- Salt and pepper to taste
- Lemon slices for garnish

DIRECTIONS:

1. Preheat the oven to 400°F (200°C). Line a baking sheet with parchment paper.
2. Place the salmon fillets on the prepared baking sheet.
3. In a small bowl, whisk together olive oil, lemon juice, minced garlic, chopped fresh dill, salt, and pepper.
4. Brush the salmon fillets with the lemon-dill mixture, coating them evenly.
5. Bake in the preheated oven for 12-15 minutes, or until the salmon is cooked through and flakes easily with a fork.
6. Serve hot, garnished with lemon slices.

2. Grilled Shrimp Skewers

INGREDIENTS:

- 1 pound large shrimp, peeled and deveined
- 2 tablespoons olive oil
- 2 cloves garlic, minced
- 1 tablespoon chopped fresh parsley
- 1 teaspoon smoked paprika
- Salt and pepper to taste
- Lemon wedges for serving

DIRECTIONS:

1. Preheat the grill to medium-high heat.
2. In a bowl, toss the shrimp with olive oil, minced garlic, chopped fresh parsley, smoked paprika, salt, and pepper until evenly coated.
3. Thread the seasoned shrimp onto skewers.
4. Grill the shrimp skewers for 2-3 minutes per side, or until they are pink and opaque.
5. Serve hot with lemon wedges for squeezing over the shrimp.

NUTRITIONAL INFORMATION (PER SERVING):

Calories: 300	
Protein: 30g	
Carbohydrates: 2g	
Fat: 20g	
Fiber: 0g	

NUTRITIONAL INFORMATION (PER SERVING):

Calories: 180	
Protein: 20g	
Carbohydrates: 1g	
Fat: 10g	
Fiber: 0g	

3. Lemon Garlic Tilapia

INGREDIENTS:

- 4 tilapia fillets (4-6 oz each)
- 2 tablespoons olive oil
- 2 cloves garlic, minced
- Zest of 1 lemon
- Juice of 1 lemon
- 1 tablespoon chopped fresh parsley
- Salt and pepper to taste

DIRECTIONS:

1. In a small bowl, whisk together olive oil, minced garlic, lemon zest, lemon juice, chopped fresh parsley, salt, and pepper.
2. Place the tilapia fillets in a shallow dish and pour the lemon-garlic mixture over them, coating evenly. Let marinate for 15-20 minutes.
3. Preheat the oven to 400°F (200°C). Line a baking sheet with parchment paper.
4. Place the marinated tilapia fillets on the prepared baking sheet.
5. Bake in the preheated oven for 12-15 minutes, or until the tilapia is cooked through and flakes easily with a fork.
6. Serve hot.

NUTRITIONAL INFORMATION (PER SERVING):

Calories: 200

Protein: 25g

Carbohydrates: 2g

Fat: 10g

Fiber: 0g

4. Seared Scallops with Garlic Butter

INGREDIENTS:

- 1 pound sea scallops
- 2 tablespoons olive oil
- 2 cloves garlic, minced
- 2 tablespoons unsalted butter
- Salt and pepper to taste
- Chopped fresh parsley for garnish
- Lemon wedges for serving

DIRECTIONS:

1. Pat the scallops dry with paper towels and season them with salt and pepper.
2. In a large skillet, heat olive oil over medium-high heat until shimmering.
3. Add the scallops to the skillet in a single layer, making sure not to overcrowd the pan. Cook for 2-3 minutes per side, or until they are golden brown and caramelized.
4. Remove the cooked scallops from the skillet and set aside.
5. In the same skillet, add minced garlic and cook until fragrant, about 1 minute.
6. Add unsalted butter to the skillet and swirl until melted and combined with the garlic.
7. Return the scallops to the skillet and toss to coat them evenly with the garlic butter sauce.
8. Serve hot, garnished with chopped fresh parsley and lemon wedges.

NUTRITIONAL INFORMATION (PER SERVING):

Calories: 200

Protein: 20g

Carbohydrates: 2g

Fat: 12g

Fiber: 0g

5. Broiled Mahi Mahi with Mango Salsa

INGREDIENTS:

- 4 mahi mahi fillets (4-6 oz each)
- 2 tablespoons olive oil
- 1 teaspoon chili powder
- 1 teaspoon ground cumin
- 1/2 teaspoon paprika
- Salt and pepper to taste

For the Mango Salsa:
- 1 ripe mango, diced
- 1/2 red onion, finely chopped
- 1/4 cup chopped fresh cilantro
- Juice of 1 lime
- Salt and pepper to taste

DIRECTIONS:

1. Preheat the broiler to high.
2. In a small bowl, combine olive oil, chili powder, ground cumin, paprika, salt, and pepper.
3. Rub the spice mixture over the mahi mahi fillets, coating them evenly.
4. Place the seasoned mahi mahi fillets on a broiler pan or baking sheet lined with aluminum foil.
5. Broil the mahi mahi fillets for 5-7 minutes per side, or until they are cooked through and flake easily with a fork.
6. Meanwhile, prepare the mango salsa by combining diced mango, finely chopped red onion, chopped fresh cilantro, lime juice, salt, and pepper in a bowl. Mix well.
7. Serve the broiled mahi mahi fillets hot, topped with mango salsa.

NUTRITIONAL INFORMATION (PER SERVING):

Calories: 250	
Protein: 30g	
Carbohydrates: 10g	
Fat: 10g	
Fiber: 2g	

6. Grilled Swordfish with Herb Butter

INGREDIENTS:

- 4 swordfish steaks (4-6 oz each)
- 2 tablespoons olive oil
- 2 cloves garlic, minced
- 1 tablespoon chopped fresh parsley
- 1 tablespoon chopped fresh basil
- 1 tablespoon chopped fresh thyme
- 2 tablespoons unsalted butter
- Salt and pepper to taste
- Lemon wedges for serving

DIRECTIONS:

1. Preheat the grill to medium-high heat.
2. In a small bowl, combine olive oil, minced garlic, chopped fresh parsley, chopped fresh basil, chopped fresh thyme, salt, and pepper.
3. Brush the swordfish steaks with the herb mixture, coating them evenly.
4. Grill the swordfish steaks for 3-4 minutes per side, or until they are cooked through and have grill marks.
5. In a small saucepan, melt unsalted butter over low heat. Add any remaining herb mixture to the melted butter and stir to combine.
6. Serve the grilled swordfish steaks hot, drizzled with herb butter and accompanied by lemon wedges.

NUTRITIONAL INFORMATION (PER SERVING):

Calories: 300	
Protein: 25g	
Carbohydrates: 2g	
Fat: 20g	
Fiber: 0g	

7. Pan-Seared Halibut with Lemon Herb Sauce

INGREDIENTS:

- 4 halibut fillets (4-6 oz each)
- 2 tablespoons olive oil
- 2 cloves garlic, minced
- Zest of 1 lemon
- Juice of 1 lemon
- 1 tablespoon chopped fresh parsley
- 1 tablespoon chopped fresh dill
- Salt and pepper to taste

For the Lemon Herb Sauce:
- 2 tablespoons unsalted butter
- 2 cloves garlic, minced
- Zest of 1 lemon
- Juice of 1 lemon
- 1 tablespoon chopped fresh parsley
- 1 tablespoon chopped fresh dill
- Salt and pepper to taste

DIRECTIONS:

1. Pat the halibut fillets dry with paper towels and season them with salt and pepper.
2. In a large skillet, heat olive oil over medium-high heat until shimmering.
3. Add the halibut fillets to the skillet and cook for 3-4 minutes per side, or until they are golden brown and cooked through.
4. Meanwhile, prepare the lemon herb sauce. In a small saucepan, melt unsalted butter over low heat. Add minced garlic and cook until fragrant, about 1 minute. Stir in lemon zest, lemon juice, chopped fresh parsley, chopped fresh dill, salt, and pepper. Cook for an additional 1-2 minutes.
5. Serve the pan-seared halibut fillets hot, drizzled with lemon herb sauce.

NUTRITIONAL INFORMATION (PER SERVING):

Calories: 280

Protein: 30g

Carbohydrates: 2g

Fat: 16g

Fiber: 0g

8. Baked Cod with Tomato and Olive Relish

INGREDIENTS:

- 4 cod fillets (4-6 oz each)
- 2 tablespoons olive oil
- 2 cloves garlic, minced
- 1 teaspoon dried oregano
- Salt and pepper to taste

For the Tomato and Olive Relish:
- 1 cup cherry tomatoes, halved
- 1/4 cup sliced Kalamata olives
- 2 tablespoons chopped fresh parsley
- 1 tablespoon olive oil
- Salt and pepper to taste

DIRECTIONS:

1. Preheat the oven to 400°F (200°C). Line a baking sheet with parchment paper.
2. Place the cod fillets on the prepared baking sheet.
3. In a small bowl, whisk together olive oil, minced garlic, dried oregano, salt, and pepper.
4. Brush the cod fillets with the olive oil mixture, coating them evenly.
5. Bake in the preheated oven for 12-15 minutes, or until the cod is cooked through and flakes easily with a fork.
6. Meanwhile, prepare the tomato and olive relish. In a bowl, combine halved cherry tomatoes, sliced Kalamata olives, chopped fresh parsley, olive oil, salt, and pepper. Mix well.
7. Serve the baked cod fillets hot, topped with tomato and olive relish.

NUTRITIONAL INFORMATION (PER SERVING):

Calories: 250

Protein: 25g

Carbohydrates: 4g

Fat: 15g

Fiber: 1g

9. Coconut Shrimp Curry

INGREDIENTS:

- 1 pound large shrimp, peeled and deveined
- 2 tablespoons olive oil
- 1 onion, diced
- 2 cloves garlic, minced
- 1 tablespoon grated ginger
- 1 red bell pepper, sliced
- 1 yellow bell pepper, sliced
- 1 can (14 oz) coconut milk
- 2 tablespoons red curry paste
- 1 tablespoon fish sauce
- 1 tablespoon lime juice
- Salt and pepper to taste
- Chopped fresh cilantro for garnish
- Cooked rice for serving

DIRECTIONS:

1. In a large skillet, heat olive oil over medium heat. Add diced onion, minced garlic, and grated ginger. Cook until softened.
2. Add sliced red bell pepper and yellow bell pepper to the skillet. Cook for 2-3 minutes.
3. Stir in coconut milk, red curry paste, fish sauce, lime juice, salt, and pepper. Bring to a simmer.
4. Add peeled and deveined shrimp to the skillet. Cook for 4-5 minutes, or until the shrimp are pink and cooked through.
5. Serve the coconut shrimp curry hot, garnished with chopped fresh cilantro, over cooked rice.

NUTRITIONAL INFORMATION (PER SERVING):

Calories:	350
Protein:	25g
Carbohydrates:	12g
Fat:	25g
Fiber:	3g

10. Tuna Salad Lettuce Wraps

INGREDIENTS:

- 2 cans (5 oz each) tuna, drained
- 1/4 cup diced celery
- 1/4 cup diced red onion
- 1/4 cup diced pickles
- 1/4 cup chopped fresh parsley
- 1/4 cup mayonnaise
- 1 tablespoon Dijon mustard
- Salt and pepper to taste
- Lettuce leaves for wrapping

DIRECTIONS:

1. In a bowl, combine drained tuna, diced celery, diced red onion, diced pickles, chopped fresh parsley, mayonnaise, Dijon mustard, salt, and pepper. Mix well.
2. Spoon the tuna salad mixture onto lettuce leaves.
3. Roll up the lettuce leaves to form wraps.
4. Serve the tuna salad lettuce wraps chilled.

NUTRITIONAL INFORMATION (PER SERVING):

Calories:	200
Protein:	20g
Carbohydrates:	4g
Fat:	12g
Fiber:	1g

11. Lemon Herb Grilled Salmon

INGREDIENTS:

- 4 salmon fillets (4-6 oz each)
- 2 tablespoons olive oil
- Zest of 1 lemon
- Juice of 1 lemon
- 1 tablespoon chopped fresh parsley
- 1 tablespoon chopped fresh dill
- Salt and pepper to taste
- Lemon wedges for serving

DIRECTIONS:

1. In a bowl, combine olive oil, lemon zest, lemon juice, chopped fresh parsley, chopped fresh dill, salt, and pepper.
2. Brush the salmon fillets with the lemon herb mixture, coating them evenly.
3. Preheat the grill to medium-high heat.
4. Grill the salmon fillets for 4-5 minutes per side, or until they are cooked through and flake easily with a fork.
5. Serve hot, garnished with lemon wedges.

🍽 NUTRITIONAL INFORMATION (PER SERVING):

Calories: 300	
Protein: 30g	
Carbohydrates: 2g	
Fat: 20g	
Fiber: 0g	

12. Spicy Garlic Shrimp Stir-Fry

INGREDIENTS:

- 1 pound large shrimp, peeled and deveined
- 2 tablespoons olive oil
- 4 cloves garlic, minced
- 1 teaspoon red pepper flakes
- 1 red bell pepper, sliced
- 1 yellow bell pepper, sliced
- 1 cup snap peas
- 2 tablespoons soy sauce
- 1 tablespoon honey
- 1 tablespoon rice vinegar
- Salt and pepper to taste
- Cooked rice for serving

DIRECTIONS:

1. In a large skillet or wok, heat olive oil over medium-high heat. Add minced garlic and red pepper flakes. Cook until fragrant, about 1 minute.
2. Add sliced red bell pepper, sliced yellow bell pepper, and snap peas to the skillet. Stir-fry for 3-4 minutes.
3. Add peeled and deveined shrimp to the skillet. Cook for 2-3 minutes, or until the shrimp are pink and cooked through.
4. In a small bowl, whisk together soy sauce, honey, rice vinegar, salt, and pepper. Pour the sauce over the shrimp and vegetables in the skillet. Stir to coat evenly.
5. Serve the spicy garlic shrimp stir-fry hot, over cooked rice.

🍽 NUTRITIONAL INFORMATION (PER SERVING):

Calories: 300	
Protein: 25g	
Carbohydrates: 20g	
Fat: 12g	
Fiber: 3g	

13. Baked Lemon Garlic Shrimp

INGREDIENTS:

- 1 pound large shrimp, peeled and deveined
- 2 tablespoons olive oil
- 4 cloves garlic, minced
- Zest of 1 lemon
- Juice of 1 lemon
- 1 tablespoon chopped fresh parsley
- Salt and pepper to taste

DIRECTIONS:

1. Preheat the oven to 400°F (200°C). Line a baking sheet with parchment paper.
2. In a bowl, toss the peeled and deveined shrimp with olive oil, minced garlic, lemon zest, lemon juice, chopped fresh parsley, salt, and pepper until evenly coated.
3. Spread the seasoned shrimp in a single layer on the prepared baking sheet.
4. Bake in the preheated oven for 8-10 minutes, or until the shrimp are pink and cooked through.
5. Serve hot.

NUTRITIONAL INFORMATION (PER SERVING):

Calories: 200	
Protein: 25g	
Carbohydrates: 2g	
Fat: 10g	
Fiber: 0g	

14. Grilled Lemon Herb Shrimp Skewers

INGREDIENTS:

- 1 pound large shrimp, peeled and deveined
- 2 tablespoons olive oil
- Zest of 1 lemon
- Juice of 1 lemon
- 1 tablespoon chopped fresh parsley
- 1 tablespoon chopped fresh dill
- Salt and pepper to taste
- Lemon wedges for serving

DIRECTIONS:

1. In a bowl, combine olive oil, lemon zest, lemon juice, chopped fresh parsley, chopped fresh dill, salt, and pepper.
2. Add the peeled and deveined shrimp to the bowl, tossing to coat them evenly with the lemon herb mixture.
3. Thread the seasoned shrimp onto skewers.
4. Preheat the grill to medium-high heat.
5. Grill the shrimp skewers for 2-3 minutes per side, or until they are pink and cooked through.
6. Serve hot, with lemon wedges for squeezing over the shrimp.

NUTRITIONAL INFORMATION (PER SERVING):

Calories: 180	
Protein: 20g	
Carbohydrates: 2g	
Fat: 10g	
Fiber: 0g	

15. Cilantro Lime Grilled Halibut

INGREDIENTS:

- 4 halibut fillets (4-6 oz each)
- 2 tablespoons olive oil
- Zest of 1 lime
- Juice of 1 lime
- 1/4 cup chopped fresh cilantro
- 2 cloves garlic, minced
- Salt and pepper to taste

DIRECTIONS:

1. In a bowl, combine olive oil, lime zest, lime juice, chopped fresh cilantro, minced garlic, salt, and pepper.
2. Brush the halibut fillets with the cilantro lime mixture, coating them evenly.
3. Preheat the grill to medium-high heat.
4. Grill the halibut fillets for 4-5 minutes per side, or until they are cooked through and flake easily with a fork.
5. Serve hot.

🍽 NUTRITIONAL INFORMATION (PER SERVING):

Calories: 250	
Protein: 30g	
Carbohydrates: 2g	
Fat: 12g	
Fiber: 0g	

16. Spicy Cajun Blackened Catfish

INGREDIENTS:

- 4 catfish fillets (4-6 oz each)
- 2 tablespoons olive oil
- 2 tablespoons Cajun seasoning
- 1 teaspoon paprika
- 1/2 teaspoon garlic powder
- 1/2 teaspoon onion powder
- Salt and pepper to taste
- Lemon wedges for serving

DIRECTIONS:

1. Pat the catfish fillets dry with paper towels and season them with Cajun seasoning, paprika, garlic powder, onion powder, salt, and pepper.
2. Heat olive oil in a large skillet over medium-high heat.
3. Add the seasoned catfish fillets to the skillet and cook for 3-4 minutes per side, or until they are blackened and cooked through.
4. Serve hot, with lemon wedges for squeezing over the catfish.

🍽 NUTRITIONAL INFORMATION (PER SERVING):

Calories: 220	
Protein: 25g	
Carbohydrates: 2g	
Fat: 12g	
Fiber: 0g	

CHAPTER 11

DESSERT AND FRUIT RECIPES

1. Berry Chia Seed Pudding

INGREDIENTS:

- 1/4 cup chia seeds
- 1 cup unsweetened almond milk
- 1 tablespoon maple syrup
- 1/2 teaspoon vanilla extract
- 1/2 cup mixed berries (such as strawberries, blueberries, and raspberries)

DIRECTIONS:

1. In a bowl, combine chia seeds, unsweetened almond milk, maple syrup, and vanilla extract. Mix well.
2. Let the mixture sit for 10 minutes, then stir again to prevent clumping.
3. Cover the bowl and refrigerate for at least 2 hours or overnight, until the chia seeds have absorbed the liquid and the mixture has thickened to a pudding-like consistency.
4. Serve the chia seed pudding topped with mixed berries.

🍽 NUTRITIONAL INFORMATION (PER SERVING):

Calories: 150	
Protein: 4g	
Carbohydrates: 20g	
Fat: 6g	
Fiber: 10g	

2. Baked Cinnamon Apples

INGREDIENTS:

- 2 apples, cored and sliced
- 1 tablespoon melted coconut oil
- 1 tablespoon maple syrup
- 1 teaspoon ground cinnamon

DIRECTIONS:

1. Preheat the oven to 375°F (190°C). Line a baking sheet with parchment paper.
2. In a bowl, toss the sliced apples with melted coconut oil, maple syrup, and ground cinnamon until evenly coated.
3. Spread the apple slices in a single layer on the prepared baking sheet.
4. Bake in the preheated oven for 20-25 minutes, or until the apples are tender and caramelized.
5. Serve the baked cinnamon apples warm.

🍽 NUTRITIONAL INFORMATION (PER SERVING):

Calories: 120	
Protein: 1g	
Carbohydrates: 25g	
Fat: 3g	
Fiber: 5g	

3. Mango Coconut Chia Popsicles

INGREDIENTS:

- 1 ripe mango, peeled and diced
- 1/2 cup coconut milk
- 2 tablespoons chia seeds
- 1 tablespoon honey or maple syrup

DIRECTIONS:

1. In a blender, puree the diced mango until smooth.
2. In a bowl, combine pureed mango, coconut milk, chia seeds, and honey or maple syrup. Mix well.
3. Pour the mixture into popsicle molds.
4. Insert popsicle sticks into the molds and freeze for at least 4 hours or until solid.
5. To unmold the popsicles, run warm water over the outside of the molds for a few seconds.
6. Serve the mango coconut chia popsicles chilled.

⟁ NUTRITIONAL INFORMATION (PER SERVING):

Calories: 100

Protein: 2g

Carbohydrates: 15g

Fat: 5g

Fiber: 4g

4. Chocolate Avocado Mousse

INGREDIENTS:

- 2 ripe avocados, peeled and pitted
- 1/4 cup unsweetened cocoa powder
- 1/4 cup maple syrup or honey
- 1 teaspoon vanilla extract
- Pinch of salt
- Optional toppings: sliced strawberries, raspberries, or shredded coconut

DIRECTIONS:

1. In a food processor or blender, combine ripe avocados, unsweetened cocoa powder, maple syrup or honey, vanilla extract, and a pinch of salt.
2. Blend until smooth and creamy, scraping down the sides of the bowl as needed.
3. Transfer the chocolate avocado mousse to serving bowls or glasses.
4. Chill in the refrigerator for at least 30 minutes before serving.
5. Serve the chocolate avocado mousse topped with sliced strawberries, raspberries, or shredded coconut if desired.

⟁ NUTRITIONAL INFORMATION (PER SERVING):

Calories: 200

Protein: 3g

Carbohydrates: 20g

Fat: 15g

Fiber: 8g

5. Pineapple Coconut Nice Cream

INGREDIENTS:

- 2 ripe bananas, peeled, sliced, and frozen
- 1 cup frozen pineapple chunks
- 1/4 cup coconut milk
- Optional toppings: toasted coconut flakes or chopped nuts

DIRECTIONS:

1. In a blender or food processor, combine frozen banana slices, frozen pineapple chunks, and coconut milk.
2. Blend until smooth and creamy, scraping down the sides of the bowl as needed.
3. Transfer the pineapple coconut nice cream to serving bowls.
4. Serve immediately, topped with toasted coconut flakes or chopped nuts if desired.

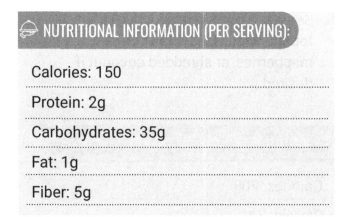

NUTRITIONAL INFORMATION (PER SERVING):

Calories: 150	
Protein: 2g	
Carbohydrates: 35g	
Fat: 1g	
Fiber: 5g	

6. Strawberry Basil Sorbet

INGREDIENTS:

- 2 cups frozen strawberries
- 1/4 cup fresh basil leaves
- 2 tablespoons honey or maple syrup
- 1 tablespoon fresh lemon juice
- 1/4 cup water

DIRECTIONS:

1. In a blender or food processor, combine frozen strawberries, fresh basil leaves, honey or maple syrup, fresh lemon juice, and water.
2. Blend until smooth, scraping down the sides of the bowl as needed.
3. Transfer the strawberry basil mixture to a shallow dish and freeze for 2-3 hours, stirring occasionally, until firm but scoopable.
4. Serve the strawberry basil sorbet chilled.

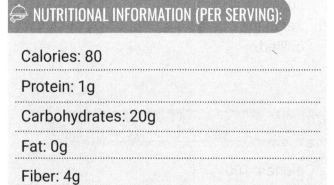

NUTRITIONAL INFORMATION (PER SERVING):

Calories: 80	
Protein: 1g	
Carbohydrates: 20g	
Fat: 0g	
Fiber: 4g	

7. Lemon Blueberry Frozen Yogurt

INGREDIENTS:

- 2 cups plain Greek yogurt
- 1 cup frozen blueberries
- Zest of 1 lemon
- 2 tablespoons honey or maple syrup

DIRECTIONS:

1. In a blender or food processor, combine plain Greek yogurt, frozen blueberries, lemon zest, and honey or maple syrup.
2. Blend until smooth and creamy, scraping down the sides of the bowl as needed.
3. Transfer the lemon blueberry frozen yogurt to a shallow dish and freeze for 2-3 hours, stirring occasionally, until firm but scoopable.
4. Serve the frozen yogurt chilled.

NUTRITIONAL INFORMATION (PER SERVING):

Calories: 120

Protein: 10g

Carbohydrates: 18g

Fat: 1g

Fiber: 2g

8. Chocolate Covered Strawberries

INGREDIENTS:

- 1 cup dark chocolate chips
- 1 tablespoon coconut oil
- 12 large strawberries, washed and dried

DIRECTIONS:

1. In a microwave-safe bowl, combine dark chocolate chips and coconut oil.
2. Microwave in 30-second intervals, stirring between each interval, until the chocolate is melted and smooth.
3. Dip each strawberry into the melted chocolate, coating it halfway.
4. Place the chocolate-covered strawberries on a parchment-lined baking sheet.
5. Refrigerate for 30 minutes, or until the chocolate is set.
6. Serve the chocolate-covered strawberries chilled.

NUTRITIONAL INFORMATION (PER SERVING):

Calories: 150

Protein: 2g

Carbohydrates: 15g

Fat: 10g

Fiber: 3g

9. Baked Cinnamon Peaches

INGREDIENTS:

- 2 ripe peaches, halved and pitted
- 1 tablespoon melted coconut oil
- 1 tablespoon honey or maple syrup
- 1/2 teaspoon ground cinnamon

DIRECTIONS:

1. Preheat the oven to 375°F (190°C). Line a baking dish with parchment paper.
2. Place the peach halves, cut side up, in the prepared baking dish.
3. In a small bowl, whisk together melted coconut oil, honey or maple syrup, and ground cinnamon.
4. Brush the peach halves with the coconut oil mixture, coating them evenly.
5. Bake in the preheated oven for 20-25 minutes, or until the peaches are tender and caramelized.
6. Serve the baked cinnamon peaches warm.

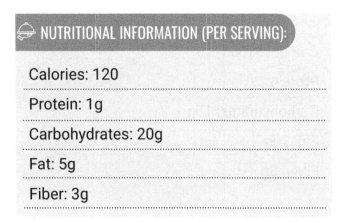

NUTRITIONAL INFORMATION (PER SERVING):

Calories: 120

Protein: 1g

Carbohydrates: 20g

Fat: 5g

Fiber: 3g

10. Coconut Mango Popsicles

INGREDIENTS:

- 1 ripe mango, peeled and diced
- 1 cup coconut water
- 2 tablespoons honey or maple syrup
- Juice of 1 lime

DIRECTIONS:

1. In a blender, puree the diced mango until smooth.
2. In a bowl, combine pureed mango, coconut water, honey or maple syrup, and lime juice. Mix well.
3. Pour the mixture into popsicle molds.
4. Insert popsicle sticks into the molds and freeze for at least 4 hours or until solid.
5. To unmold the popsicles, run warm water over the outside of the molds for a few seconds.
6. Serve the coconut mango popsicles chilled.

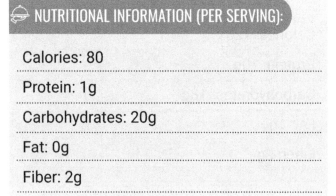

NUTRITIONAL INFORMATION (PER SERVING):

Calories: 80

Protein: 1g

Carbohydrates: 20g

Fat: 0g

Fiber: 2g

11. Almond Butter Banana Bites

INGREDIENTS:

- 2 bananas, peeled and sliced
- 1/4 cup almond butter
- 2 tablespoons unsweetened shredded coconut
- 2 tablespoons chopped nuts (such as almonds or walnuts)

DIRECTIONS:

1. Spread almond butter on one side of each banana slice.
2. Sprinkle unsweetened shredded coconut and chopped nuts over the almond butter.
3. Serve immediately, or refrigerate for 30 minutes to allow the almond butter to firm up slightly.

 **NUTRITIONAL INFORMATION (PER SERVING):**

Calories: 150

Protein: 3g

Carbohydrates: 15g

Fat: 10g

Fiber: 3g

12. Honey Roasted Peaches with Greek Yogurt

INGREDIENTS:

- 2 ripe peaches, halved and pitted
- 2 tablespoons honey
- 1/4 teaspoon ground cinnamon
- 1 cup plain Greek yogurt

DIRECTIONS:

1. Preheat the oven to 400°F (200°C). Line a baking dish with parchment paper.
2. Place the peach halves, cut side up, in the prepared baking dish.
3. Drizzle honey over the peach halves and sprinkle with ground cinnamon.
4. Bake in the preheated oven for 20-25 minutes, or until the peaches are tender and caramelized.
5. Serve the honey roasted peaches warm, with a dollop of plain Greek yogurt on top.

NUTRITIONAL INFORMATION (PER SERVING):

Calories: 180

Protein: 10g

Carbohydrates: 25g

Fat: 5g

Fiber: 3g

13. Chocolate Banana Nice Cream

INGREDIENTS:

- 2 ripe bananas, peeled, sliced, and frozen
- 2 tablespoons unsweetened cocoa powder
- 1 tablespoon honey or maple syrup
- 1/4 teaspoon vanilla extract

DIRECTIONS:

1. In a blender or food processor, combine frozen banana slices, unsweetened cocoa powder, honey or maple syrup, and vanilla extract.
2. Blend until smooth and creamy, scraping down the sides of the bowl as needed.
3. Serve the chocolate banana nice cream immediately, or freeze for 1-2 hours for a firmer texture.

🍽 NUTRITIONAL INFORMATION (PER SERVING):

Calories: 150

Protein: 2g

Carbohydrates: 35g

Fat: 1g

Fiber: 5g

14. Kiwi Lime Sorbet

INGREDIENTS:

- 4 kiwi fruits, peeled and diced
- Juice of 2 limes
- 2 tablespoons honey or maple syrup
- 1/4 cup water

DIRECTIONS:

1. In a blender or food processor, combine diced kiwi fruits, lime juice, honey or maple syrup, and water.
2. Blend until smooth, scraping down the sides of the bowl as needed.
3. Transfer the kiwi lime mixture to a shallow dish and freeze for 2-3 hours, stirring occasionally, until firm but scoopable.
4. Serve the kiwi lime sorbet chilled.

🍽 NUTRITIONAL INFORMATION (PER SERVING):

Calories: 100

Protein: 1g

Carbohydrates: 25g

Fat: 0g

Fiber: 5g

15. Mixed Berry Yogurt Parfait

INGREDIENTS:

- 1 cup mixed berries (such as strawberries, blueberries, and raspberries)
- 1 cup plain Greek yogurt
- 2 tablespoons honey or maple syrup
- 1/4 cup granola

DIRECTIONS:

1. In a bowl, combine mixed berries with honey or maple syrup. Mix well.
2. In serving glasses or bowls, layer plain Greek yogurt, mixed berries, and granola.
3. Repeat the layers until the glasses or bowls are filled.
4. Serve the mixed berry yogurt parfait immediately.

🔔 NUTRITIONAL INFORMATION (PER SERVING):

Calories: 200	
Protein: 10g	
Carbohydrates: 30g	
Fat: 5g	
Fiber: 5g	

16. Grilled Pineapple with Honey Lime Glaze

INGREDIENTS:

- 1 ripe pineapple, peeled, cored, and sliced into rings
- 2 tablespoons honey
- Juice of 1 lime
- Fresh mint leaves for garnish

DIRECTIONS:

1. Preheat the grill to medium-high heat.
2. In a small bowl, whisk together honey and lime juice to make the glaze.
3. Brush both sides of pineapple slices with the honey lime glaze.
4. Grill the pineapple slices for 2-3 minutes per side, or until they are caramelized and grill marks appear.
5. Serve the grilled pineapple hot, garnished with fresh mint leaves.

🔔 NUTRITIONAL INFORMATION (PER SERVING):

Calories: 100	
Protein: 1g	
Carbohydrates: 25g	
Fat: 0g	
Fiber: 3g	

CHAPTER 12
VEGETARIAN RECIPES

1. Quinoa Stuffed Bell Peppers

INGREDIENTS:

- 4 large bell peppers, halved and seeds removed
- 1 cup quinoa, rinsed
- 2 cups vegetable broth
- 1 can (15 oz) black beans, drained and rinsed
- 1 cup corn kernels (fresh or frozen)
- 1 cup diced tomatoes
- 1/2 cup diced red onion
- 1/2 cup diced bell pepper
- 2 cloves garlic, minced
- 1 teaspoon ground cumin
- 1 teaspoon chili powder
- Salt and pepper to taste
- Optional toppings: chopped cilantro, avocado slices, shredded cheese

DIRECTIONS:

1. Preheat the oven to 375°F (190°C). Arrange the bell pepper halves in a baking dish.
2. In a saucepan, bring the vegetable broth to a boil. Add quinoa, reduce heat to low, cover, and simmer for 15 minutes or until quinoa is cooked and liquid is absorbed.
3. In a large bowl, combine cooked quinoa, black beans, corn kernels, diced tomatoes, diced red onion, diced bell pepper, minced garlic, ground cumin, chili powder, salt, and pepper. Mix well.
4. Stuff each bell pepper half with the quinoa mixture, pressing down gently to pack it.
5. Cover the baking dish with aluminium foil and bake for 25-30 minutes, or until the bell peppers are tender.
6. Remove from the oven and serve hot, topped with optional toppings if desired.

2. Lentil Spinach Curry

INGREDIENTS:

- 1 cup dried green or brown lentils, rinsed
- 2 cups vegetable broth
- 1 tablespoon olive oil
- 1 onion, diced
- 2 cloves garlic, minced
- 1 tablespoon grated ginger
- 1 tablespoon curry powder
- 1 teaspoon ground turmeric
- 1 teaspoon ground cumin
- 1/2 teaspoon ground coriander
- 1 can (14 oz) diced tomatoes
- 1 can (14 oz) coconut milk
- 2 cups fresh spinach leaves
- Salt and pepper to taste
- Cooked rice for serving

DIRECTIONS:

1. In a saucepan, combine rinsed lentils and vegetable broth. Bring to a boil, then reduce heat to low, cover, and simmer for 20-25 minutes, or until lentils are tender and most of the liquid is absorbed.
2. In a large skillet, heat olive oil over medium heat. Add diced onion, minced garlic, and grated ginger. Cook until softened.
3. Stir in curry powder, ground turmeric, ground cumin, and ground coriander. Cook for 1-2 minutes, until fragrant.
4. Add diced tomatoes (with their juices) and coconut milk to the skillet. Bring to a simmer.
5. Add cooked lentils and fresh spinach leaves to the skillet. Cook until spinach wilts and flavors are combined, about 5 minutes.
6. Season with salt and pepper to taste.
7. Serve the lentil spinach curry hot, over cooked rice.

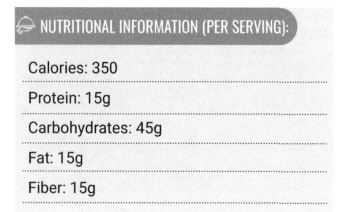

🍽 NUTRITIONAL INFORMATION (PER SERVING):	🍽 NUTRITIONAL INFORMATION (PER SERVING):
Calories: 300	Calories: 350
Protein: 12g	Protein: 15g
Carbohydrates: 55g	Carbohydrates: 45g
Fat: 3g	Fat: 15g
Fiber: 10g	Fiber: 15g

3. Vegetable Stir-Fry with Tofu

INGREDIENTS:

- 1 block (14 oz) extra-firm tofu, pressed and cubed
- 2 tablespoons soy sauce
- 1 tablespoon sesame oil
- 1 tablespoon olive oil
- 2 cloves garlic, minced
- 1 tablespoon grated ginger
- 1 bell pepper, thinly sliced
- 1 cup sliced mushrooms
- 1 cup broccoli florets
- 1 cup snow peas
- 1 carrot, julienned
- Salt and pepper to taste
- Cooked rice or quinoa for serving

DIRECTIONS:

1. In a bowl, toss cubed tofu with soy sauce and sesame oil. Let marinate for 15 minutes.
2. Heat olive oil in a large skillet or wok over medium-high heat. Add minced garlic and grated ginger. Cook until fragrant.
3. Add marinated tofu to the skillet. Cook until browned on all sides.
4. Add sliced bell pepper, sliced mushrooms, broccoli florets, snow peas, and julienned carrot to the skillet. Stir-fry until vegetables are tender-crisp.
5. Season with salt and pepper to taste.
6. Serve the vegetable stir-fry with tofu hot, over cooked rice or quinoa.

NUTRITIONAL INFORMATION (PER SERVING):

Calories: 300

Protein: 20g

Carbohydrates: 25g

Fat: 15g

Fiber: 8g

4. Chickpea Spinach Salad

INGREDIENTS:

- 1 can (15 oz) chickpeas, drained and rinsed
- 2 cups fresh spinach leaves
- 1 cup cherry tomatoes, halved
- 1/2 cucumber, diced
- 1/4 cup diced red onion
- 1/4 cup chopped fresh parsley
- 2 tablespoons olive oil
- 1 tablespoon lemon juice
- 1 teaspoon Dijon mustard
- Salt and pepper to taste
- Optional toppings: crumbled feta cheese, toasted pine nuts

DIRECTIONS:

1. In a large bowl, combine drained and rinsed chickpeas, fresh spinach leaves, halved cherry tomatoes, diced cucumber, diced red onion, and chopped fresh parsley.
2. In a small bowl, whisk together olive oil, lemon juice, Dijon mustard, salt, and pepper to make the dressing.
3. Pour the dressing over the salad ingredients in the large bowl. Toss to coat evenly.
4. Serve the chickpea spinach salad cold, topped with optional toppings if desired.

NUTRITIONAL INFORMATION (PER SERVING):

Calories: 250

Protein: 10g

Carbohydrates: 30g

Fat: 10g

Fiber: 8g

5. Eggplant and Zucchini Ratatouille

INGREDIENTS:

- 1 eggplant, diced
- 2 zucchini, diced
- 1 onion, diced
- 2 cloves garlic, minced
- 1 can (14 oz) diced tomatoes
- 2 tablespoons tomato paste
- 1 teaspoon dried thyme
- 1 teaspoon dried oregano
- Salt and pepper to taste
- Fresh basil leaves for garnish

DIRECTIONS:

1. Heat olive oil in a large skillet or Dutch oven over medium heat. Add diced eggplant and diced zucchini. Cook until lightly browned.
2. Add diced onion and minced garlic to the skillet. Cook until softened.
3. Stir in diced tomatoes, tomato paste, dried thyme, dried oregano, salt, and pepper.
4. Reduce heat to low, cover, and simmer for 20-25 minutes, stirring occasionally, until vegetables are tender and flavors are combined.
5. Serve the eggplant and zucchini ratatouille hot, garnished with fresh basil leaves.

🍽 NUTRITIONAL INFORMATION (PER SERVING):

Calories: 200	
Protein: 5g	
Carbohydrates: 35g	
Fat: 5g	
Fiber: 10g	

6. Sweet Potato and Black Bean Tacos

INGREDIENTS:

- 2 large sweet potatoes, peeled and diced
- 1 tablespoon olive oil
- 1 teaspoon chili powder
- 1 teaspoon ground cumin
- 1/2 teaspoon paprika
- Salt and pepper to taste
- 1 can (15 oz) black beans, drained and rinsed
- 1/2 cup diced red onion
- 1/4 cup chopped fresh cilantro
- 8 small corn tortillas
- Optional toppings: diced avocado, salsa, lime wedges

DIRECTIONS:

1. Preheat the oven to 400°F (200°C). Line a baking sheet with parchment paper.
2. In a bowl, toss diced sweet potatoes with olive oil, chili powder, ground cumin, paprika, salt, and pepper until evenly coated.
3. Spread the seasoned sweet potatoes in a single layer on the prepared baking sheet.
4. Roast in the preheated oven for 20-25 minutes, or until the sweet potatoes are tender and lightly browned.
5. In a skillet, heat black beans over medium heat until warmed through.
6. Warm corn tortillas in a dry skillet or microwave.
7. Assemble the tacos by filling each tortilla with roasted sweet potatoes, warmed black beans, diced red onion, and chopped fresh cilantro.
8. Serve the sweet potato and black bean tacos hot, with optional toppings if desired.

🍽 NUTRITIONAL INFORMATION (PER SERVING):

Calories: 250	
Protein: 8g	
Carbohydrates: 45g	
Fat: 5g	
Fiber: 10g	

7. Spinach and Mushroom Quiche

INGREDIENTS:

- 1 prepared pie crust (store-bought or homemade)
- 1 tablespoon olive oil
- 1 onion, diced
- 8 oz mushrooms, sliced
- 2 cups fresh spinach leaves
- 4 large eggs
- 1 cup milk or unsweetened almond milk
- 1/2 cup shredded cheese (such as Swiss or Gruyere)
- Salt and pepper to taste
- Pinch of nutmeg

DIRECTIONS:

1. Preheat the oven to 375°F (190°C). Place the prepared pie crust in a pie dish and set aside.
2. In a skillet, heat olive oil over medium heat. Add diced onion and sliced mushrooms. Cook until softened.
3. Add fresh spinach leaves to the skillet and cook until wilted.
4. In a bowl, whisk together eggs, milk, shredded cheese, salt, pepper, and nutmeg.
5. Spread the cooked vegetables evenly over the bottom of the pie crust.
6. Pour the egg mixture over the vegetables in the pie crust.
7. Bake in the preheated oven for 30-35 minutes, or until the quiche is set and golden brown on top.
8. Remove from the oven and let cool slightly before slicing and serving.

NUTRITIONAL INFORMATION (PER SERVING):

Calories: 300

Protein: 12g

Carbohydrates: 20g

Fat: 18g

Fiber: 3g

8. Spaghetti Squash Primavera

INGREDIENTS:

- 1 medium spaghetti squash
- 1 tablespoon olive oil
- 1 onion, diced
- 2 cloves garlic, minced
- 1 bell pepper, diced
- 1 cup cherry tomatoes, halved
- 1 cup sliced mushrooms
- 2 cups fresh spinach leaves
- Salt and pepper to taste
- Grated Parmesan cheese for serving (optional)

DIRECTIONS:

1. Preheat the oven to 375°F (190°C). Cut the spaghetti squash in half lengthwise and scoop out the seeds.
2. Place the spaghetti squash halves, cut side down, on a baking sheet lined with parchment paper.
3. Bake in the preheated oven for 40-45 minutes, or until the squash is tender and easily pierced with a fork.
4. Remove the squash from the oven and let cool slightly. Use a fork to scrape the flesh into spaghetti-like strands.
5. In a large skillet, heat olive oil over medium heat. Add diced onion and minced garlic. Cook until softened.
6. Add diced bell pepper, halved cherry tomatoes, sliced mushrooms, and fresh spinach leaves to the skillet. Cook until vegetables are tender-crisp.
7. Season with salt and pepper to taste.
8. Toss the cooked spaghetti squash strands with the vegetable mixture in the skillet.
9. Serve the spaghetti squash primavera hot, with grated Parmesan cheese if desired.

NUTRITIONAL INFORMATION (PER SERVING):

Calories: 200

Protein: 5g

Carbohydrates: 30g

Fat: 8g

Fiber: 8g

9. Veggie and Hummus Wrap

INGREDIENTS:

- 4 large whole wheat tortillas
- 1 cup hummus
- 2 cups mixed salad greens
- 1 bell pepper, thinly sliced
- 1/2 cucumber, thinly sliced
- 1/4 cup shredded carrots
- 1/4 cup thinly sliced red cabbage
- Salt and pepper to taste

DIRECTIONS:

1. Spread a generous layer of hummus over each whole wheat tortilla.
2. Place mixed salad greens, thinly sliced bell pepper, thinly sliced cucumber, shredded carrots, and thinly sliced red cabbage on top of the hummus.
3. Season with salt and pepper to taste.
4. Roll up the tortillas tightly, tucking in the sides as you go.
5. Slice the veggie and hummus wraps in half diagonally.
6. Serve the wraps immediately, or wrap tightly in plastic wrap and refrigerate for later.

NUTRITIONAL INFORMATION (PER SERVING):

Calories:	300
Protein:	10g
Carbohydrates:	45g
Fat:	10g
Fiber:	8g

10. Spinach and Feta Stuffed Portobello Mushrooms

INGREDIENTS:

- 4 large portobello mushrooms, stems removed
- 2 tablespoons olive oil
- 2 cloves garlic, minced
- 2 cups fresh spinach leaves
- 1/2 cup crumbled feta cheese
- Salt and pepper to taste
- Fresh parsley for garnish

DIRECTIONS:

1. Preheat the oven to 375°F (190°C). Line a baking sheet with parchment paper.
2. Place portobello mushrooms, stem side up, on the prepared baking sheet.
3. In a skillet, heat olive oil over medium heat. Add minced garlic and cook until fragrant.
4. Add fresh spinach leaves to the skillet and cook until wilted.
5. Remove the skillet from heat and stir in crumbled feta cheese. Season with salt and pepper to taste.
6. Divide the spinach and feta mixture evenly among the portobello mushrooms, filling the caps.
7. Bake in the preheated oven for 20-25 minutes, or until the mushrooms are tender and the filling is heated through.
8. Remove from the oven and garnish with fresh parsley before serving.

NUTRITIONAL INFORMATION (PER SERVING):

Calories:	200
Protein:	10g
Carbohydrates:	10g
Fat:	15g
Fiber:	3g

11. Butternut Squash and Lentil Soup

INGREDIENTS:

- 1 tablespoon olive oil
- 1 onion, diced
- 2 cloves garlic, minced
- 2 carrots, diced
- 2 stalks celery, diced
- 1 butternut squash, peeled, seeded, and diced
- 1 cup dried green or brown lentils, rinsed
- 6 cups vegetable broth
- 1 teaspoon dried thyme
- Salt and pepper to taste
- Fresh parsley for garnish

DIRECTIONS:

1. In a large pot, heat olive oil over medium heat. Add diced onion and minced garlic. Cook until softened.
2. Add diced carrots, diced celery, diced butternut squash, and rinsed lentils to the pot. Cook for a few minutes, stirring occasionally.
3. Pour vegetable broth into the pot. Add dried thyme, salt, and pepper.
4. Bring the soup to a boil, then reduce heat to low, cover, and simmer for 20-25 minutes, or until the vegetables and lentils are tender.
5. Use an immersion blender to blend the soup until smooth, or blend in batches in a regular blender until smooth.
6. Adjust seasoning if necessary.
7. Serve the butternut squash and lentil soup hot, garnished with fresh parsley.

🍽 NUTRITIONAL INFORMATION (PER SERVING):

Calories: 250

Protein: 10g

Carbohydrates: 45g

Fat: 5g

Fiber: 12g

12. Mediterranean Chickpea Salad

INGREDIENTS:

- 2 cans (15 oz each) chickpeas, drained and rinsed
- 1 cup cherry tomatoes, halved
- 1 cucumber, diced
- 1/2 red onion, thinly sliced
- 1/4 cup chopped fresh parsley
- 1/4 cup chopped fresh mint
- 1/4 cup sliced Kalamata olives
- 1/4 cup crumbled feta cheese
- 2 tablespoons olive oil
- 1 tablespoon red wine vinegar
- Salt and pepper to taste

DIRECTIONS:

1. In a large bowl, combine drained and rinsed chickpeas, halved cherry tomatoes, diced cucumber, thinly sliced red onion, chopped fresh parsley, chopped fresh mint, sliced Kalamata olives, and crumbled feta cheese.
2. In a small bowl, whisk together olive oil, red wine vinegar, salt, and pepper to make the dressing.
3. Pour the dressing over the salad ingredients in the large bowl. Toss to coat evenly.
4. Serve the Mediterranean chickpea salad cold, as a side dish or a main course.

🍽 NUTRITIONAL INFORMATION (PER SERVING):

Calories: 300

Protein: 15g

Carbohydrates: 35g

Fat: 12g

Fiber: 10g

13. Caprese Quinoa Salad

INGREDIENTS:

- 1 cup quinoa, rinsed
- 2 cups water
- 1 cup cherry tomatoes, halved
- 1 ball fresh mozzarella, diced
- 1/4 cup chopped fresh basil
- 2 tablespoons olive oil
- 1 tablespoon balsamic vinegar
- Salt and pepper to taste

DIRECTIONS:

1. In a saucepan, combine rinsed quinoa and water. Bring to a boil, then reduce heat to low, cover, and simmer for 15-20 minutes, or until quinoa is cooked and water is absorbed.
2. Fluff cooked quinoa with a fork and let cool slightly.
3. In a large bowl, combine cooked quinoa, halved cherry tomatoes, diced fresh mozzarella, and chopped fresh basil.
4. In a small bowl, whisk together olive oil, balsamic vinegar, salt, and pepper to make the dressing.
5. Pour the dressing over the quinoa salad in the large bowl. Toss to coat evenly.
6. Serve the Caprese quinoa salad cold, as a side dish or a main course.

🍽 NUTRITIONAL INFORMATION (PER SERVING):

Calories: 300	
Protein: 12g	
Carbohydrates: 30g	
Fat: 15g	
Fiber: 5g	

14. Tofu and Vegetable Stir-Fry

INGREDIENTS:

- 1 block (14 oz) extra-firm tofu, pressed and cubed
- 2 tablespoons soy sauce
- 1 tablespoon cornstarch
- 2 tablespoons olive oil
- 2 cloves garlic, minced
- 1 tablespoon grated ginger
- 1 bell pepper, thinly sliced
- 1 cup sliced mushrooms
- 1 cup broccoli florets
- 1 cup snow peas
- 1 carrot, julienned
- Salt and pepper to taste
- Cooked rice or quinoa for serving

DIRECTIONS:

1. In a bowl, toss cubed tofu with soy sauce and cornstarch until evenly coated. Let marinate for 15 minutes.
2. Heat olive oil in a large skillet or wok over medium-high heat. Add minced garlic and grated ginger. Cook until fragrant.
3. Add marinated tofu to the skillet. Cook until browned on all sides.
4. Add thinly sliced bell pepper, sliced mushrooms, broccoli florets, snow peas, and julienned carrot to the skillet. Stir-fry until vegetables are tender-crisp.
5. Season with salt and pepper to taste.
6. Serve the tofu and vegetable stir-fry hot, over cooked rice or quinoa.

🍽 NUTRITIONAL INFORMATION (PER SERVING):

Calories: 300	
Protein: 20g	
Carbohydrates: 25g	
Fat: 15g	
Fiber: 8g	

15. Black Bean and Sweet Potato Enchiladas

INGREDIENTS:

- 2 large sweet potatoes, peeled and diced
- 1 tablespoon olive oil
- 1 teaspoon chili powder
- 1 teaspoon ground cumin
- Salt and pepper to taste
- 1 can (15 oz) black beans, drained and rinsed
- 1 cup diced tomatoes
- 1 cup diced red onion
- 1/4 cup chopped fresh cilantro
- 8 small corn tortillas
- 1 cup enchilada sauce
- 1/2 cup shredded cheese (such as cheddar or Monterey Jack)
- Optional toppings: diced avocado, sliced jalapenos, chopped green onions

DIRECTIONS:

1. Preheat the oven to 375°F (190°C). Line a baking sheet with parchment paper.
2. In a bowl, toss diced sweet potatoes with olive oil, chili powder, ground cumin, salt, and pepper until evenly coated.
3. Spread the seasoned sweet potatoes in a single layer on the prepared baking sheet.
4. Roast in the preheated oven for 20-25 minutes, or until the sweet potatoes are tender and lightly browned.
5. In a large bowl, combine roasted sweet potatoes, drained and rinsed black beans, diced tomatoes, diced red onion, and chopped fresh cilantro.
6. Warm corn tortillas in a dry skillet or microwave.
7. Spread a spoonful of enchilada sauce in the bottom of a baking dish.
8. Fill each warmed corn tortilla with the sweet potato and black bean mixture. Roll up and place seam side down in the baking dish.
9. Pour the remaining enchilada sauce over the filled tortillas. Sprinkle shredded cheese on top.
10. Bake in the preheated oven for 20-25 minutes, or until the enchiladas are heated through and the cheese is melted and bubbly.
11. Serve the black bean and sweet potato enchiladas hot, with optional toppings if desired.

⏱ NUTRITIONAL INFORMATION (PER SERVING):

Calories: 350

Protein: 12g

Carbohydrates: 45g

Fat: 15g

Fiber: 10g

16. Mediterranean Stuffed Peppers

INGREDIENTS:

- 4 large bell peppers, halved and seeds removed
- 1 cup cooked quinoa
- 1 can (15 oz) chickpeas, drained and rinsed
- 1 cup diced tomatoes
- 1/2 cup diced red onion
- 1/4 cup sliced Kalamata olives
- 1/4 cup crumbled feta cheese
- 2 tablespoons chopped fresh parsley
- 2 tablespoons olive oil
- 1 tablespoon balsamic vinegar
- Salt and pepper to taste

DIRECTIONS:

1. Preheat the oven to 375°F (190°C). Arrange the bell pepper halves in a baking dish.
2. In a large bowl, combine cooked quinoa, drained and rinsed chickpeas, diced tomatoes, diced red onion, sliced Kalamata olives, crumbled feta cheese, chopped fresh parsley, olive oil, balsamic vinegar, salt, and pepper. Mix well.
3. Stuff each bell pepper half with the quinoa mixture, pressing down gently to pack it.
4. Cover the baking dish with aluminum foil and bake for 25-30 minutes, or until the bell peppers are tender.
5. Remove from the oven and serve hot.

⏱ NUTRITIONAL INFORMATION (PER SERVING):

Calories: 300

Protein: 10g

Carbohydrates: 40g

Fat: 10g

Fiber: 10g

CHAPTER 13
SIDE DISHES RECIPES

1. Roasted Garlic Cauliflower

INGREDIENTS:

- 1 head cauliflower, cut into florets
- 2 tablespoons olive oil
- 4 cloves garlic, minced
- Salt and pepper to taste
- Fresh parsley for garnish

DIRECTIONS:

1. Preheat the oven to 425°F (220°C). Line a baking sheet with parchment paper.
2. In a large bowl, toss cauliflower florets with olive oil and minced garlic until evenly coated.
3. Spread the cauliflower in a single layer on the prepared baking sheet.
4. Season with salt and pepper to taste.
5. Roast in the preheated oven for 20-25 minutes, or until the cauliflower is tender and lightly browned.
6. Remove from the oven and garnish with fresh parsley before serving.

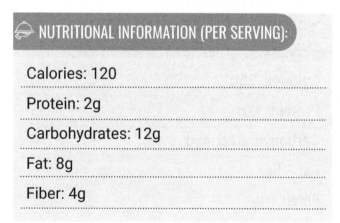

🍽 NUTRITIONAL INFORMATION (PER SERVING):

Calories: 100	
Protein: 3g	
Carbohydrates: 8g	
Fat: 7g	
Fiber: 4g	

2. Turmeric Roasted Carrots

INGREDIENTS:

- 1 pound carrots, peeled and sliced into sticks
- 2 tablespoons olive oil
- 1 teaspoon ground turmeric
- 1 teaspoon ground cumin
- Salt and pepper to taste
- Fresh cilantro for garnish

DIRECTIONS:

1. Preheat the oven to 400°F (200°C). Line a baking sheet with parchment paper.
2. In a large bowl, toss carrot sticks with olive oil, ground turmeric, ground cumin, salt, and pepper until evenly coated.
3. Spread the seasoned carrots in a single layer on the prepared baking sheet.
4. Roast in the preheated oven for 20-25 minutes, or until the carrots are tender and caramelized.
5. Remove from the oven and garnish with fresh cilantro before serving.

🍽 NUTRITIONAL INFORMATION (PER SERVING):

Calories: 120	
Protein: 2g	
Carbohydrates: 12g	
Fat: 8g	
Fiber: 4g	

3. Lemon Garlic Broccoli

INGREDIENTS:

- 1 pound broccoli florets
- 2 tablespoons olive oil
- Zest and juice of 1 lemon
- 4 cloves garlic, minced
- Salt and pepper to taste
- Lemon wedges for serving

DIRECTIONS:

1. Steam broccoli florets until tender-crisp, about 5 minutes. Drain and set aside.
2. In a large skillet, heat olive oil over medium heat. Add minced garlic and cook until fragrant.
3. Add steamed broccoli florets to the skillet. Stir in lemon zest and lemon juice.
4. Cook for 2-3 minutes, tossing occasionally, until broccoli is coated in the lemon garlic mixture.
5. Season with salt and pepper to taste.
6. Serve the lemon garlic broccoli hot, with lemon wedges on the side.

🍽 NUTRITIONAL INFORMATION (PER SERVING):

Calories: 80

Protein: 3g

Carbohydrates: 10g

Fat: 5g

Fiber: 4g

4. Balsamic Roasted Brussels Sprouts

INGREDIENTS:

- 1 pound Brussels sprouts, trimmed and halved
- 2 tablespoons olive oil
- 2 tablespoons balsamic vinegar
- 1 tablespoon maple syrup
- Salt and pepper to taste
- Toasted walnuts for garnish (optional)

DIRECTIONS:

1. Preheat the oven to 400°F (200°C). Line a baking sheet with parchment paper.
2. In a large bowl, toss Brussels sprouts with olive oil, balsamic vinegar, maple syrup, salt, and pepper until evenly coated.
3. Spread the seasoned Brussels sprouts in a single layer on the prepared baking sheet.
4. Roast in the preheated oven for 20-25 minutes, or until the Brussels sprouts are tender and caramelized.
5. Remove from the oven and garnish with toasted walnuts before serving.

🍽 NUTRITIONAL INFORMATION (PER SERVING):

Calories: 100

Protein: 4g

Carbohydrates: 12g

Fat: 5g

Fiber: 4g

5. Quinoa and Black Bean Salad

INGREDIENTS:

- 1 cup cooked quinoa
- 1 can (15 oz) black beans, drained and rinsed
- 1 cup diced cucumber
- 1 cup halved cherry tomatoes
- 1/4 cup diced red onion
- 1/4 cup chopped fresh cilantro
- 2 tablespoons olive oil
- 2 tablespoons lime juice
- Salt and pepper to taste

DIRECTIONS:

1. In a large bowl, combine cooked quinoa, drained and rinsed black beans, diced cucumber, halved cherry tomatoes, diced red onion, and chopped fresh cilantro.
2. In a small bowl, whisk together olive oil, lime juice, salt, and pepper to make the dressing.
3. Pour the dressing over the salad ingredients in the large bowl. Toss to coat evenly.
4. Serve the quinoa and black bean salad cold or at room temperature.

🛎 NUTRITIONAL INFORMATION (PER SERVING):

Calories: 200	
Protein: 8g	
Carbohydrates: 30g	
Fat: 8g	
Fiber: 8g	

6. Garlic Herb Roasted Potatoes

INGREDIENTS:

- 1 pound baby potatoes, halved
- 2 tablespoons olive oil
- 4 cloves garlic, minced
- 1 tablespoon chopped fresh rosemary
- 1 tablespoon chopped fresh thyme
- Salt and pepper to taste
- Chopped fresh parsley for garnish

DIRECTIONS:

1. Preheat the oven to 425°F (220°C). Line a baking sheet with parchment paper.
2. In a large bowl, toss halved baby potatoes with olive oil, minced garlic, chopped fresh rosemary, chopped fresh thyme, salt, and pepper until evenly coated.
3. Spread the seasoned potatoes in a single layer on the prepared baking sheet.
4. Roast in the preheated oven for 25-30 minutes, or until the potatoes are tender and golden brown.
5. Remove from the oven and garnish with chopped fresh parsley before serving.

🛎 NUTRITIONAL INFORMATION (PER SERVING):

Calories: 150	
Protein: 3g	
Carbohydrates: 20g	
Fat: 7g	
Fiber: 3g	

7. Grilled Asparagus with Lemon Zest

INGREDIENTS:

- 1 pound asparagus spears, trimmed
- 2 tablespoons olive oil
- Zest of 1 lemon
- Salt and pepper to taste
- Lemon wedges for serving

DIRECTIONS:

1. Preheat a grill or grill pan over medium-high heat.
2. In a large bowl, toss trimmed asparagus spears with olive oil until evenly coated.
3. Place the asparagus spears on the preheated grill and cook for 3-4 minutes per side, or until tender and slightly charred.
4. Transfer grilled asparagus to a serving platter.
5. Sprinkle lemon zest over the grilled asparagus and season with salt and pepper to taste.
6. Serve hot, with lemon wedges on the side.

NUTRITIONAL INFORMATION (PER SERVING):

Calories: 80	
Protein: 4g	
Carbohydrates: 6g	
Fat: 6g	
Fiber: 3g	

8. Lemon Herb Quinoa Pilaf

INGREDIENTS:

- 1 cup cooked quinoa
- Zest and juice of 1 lemon
- 2 tablespoons chopped fresh parsley
- 1 tablespoon chopped fresh dill
- 1 tablespoon chopped fresh chives
- Salt and pepper to taste

DIRECTIONS:

1. In a bowl, combine cooked quinoa, lemon zest, lemon juice, chopped fresh parsley, chopped fresh dill, and chopped fresh chives.
2. Season with salt and pepper to taste.
3. Toss to combine all ingredients thoroughly.
4. Serve the lemon herb quinoa pilaf warm or at room temperature.

NUTRITIONAL INFORMATION (PER SERVING):

Calories: 150	
Protein: 4g	
Carbohydrates: 25g	
Fat: 5g	
Fiber: 3g	

9. Cucumber Avocado Salad

INGREDIENTS:

- 2 cucumbers, thinly sliced
- 1 ripe avocado, diced
- 1/4 cup thinly sliced red onion
- 2 tablespoons chopped fresh dill
- 2 tablespoons olive oil
- 1 tablespoon white wine vinegar
- Salt and pepper to taste

DIRECTIONS:

1. In a large bowl, combine thinly sliced cucumbers, diced avocado, thinly sliced red onion, and chopped fresh dill.
2. In a small bowl, whisk together olive oil, white wine vinegar, salt, and pepper to make the dressing.
3. Pour the dressing over the salad ingredients in the large bowl. Toss to coat evenly.
4. Serve the cucumber avocado salad cold or at room temperature.

NUTRITIONAL INFORMATION (PER SERVING):

Calories: 200	
Protein: 4g	
Carbohydrates: 15g	
Fat: 15g	
Fiber: 8g	

10. Roasted Beet and Arugula Salad

INGREDIENTS:

- 2 large beets, peeled and diced
- 2 tablespoons olive oil
- Salt and pepper to taste
- 4 cups arugula
- 1/4 cup crumbled goat cheese
- 1/4 cup chopped walnuts
- Balsamic glaze for drizzling

DIRECTIONS:

1. Preheat the oven to 400°F (200°C). Line a baking sheet with parchment paper.
2. In a bowl, toss diced beets with olive oil, salt, and pepper until evenly coated.
3. Spread the seasoned beets in a single layer on the prepared baking sheet.
4. Roast in the preheated oven for 30-35 minutes, or until the beets are tender and caramelized.
5. Remove from the oven and let cool slightly.
6. In a large bowl, combine roasted beets and arugula.
7. Sprinkle crumbled goat cheese and chopped walnuts over the salad.
8. Drizzle with balsamic glaze before serving.

NUTRITIONAL INFORMATION (PER SERVING):

Calories: 250	
Protein: 8g	
Carbohydrates: 20g	
Fat: 15g	
Fiber: 6g	

11. Sauteed Garlic Kale

INGREDIENTS:

- 1 bunch kale, stems removed and leaves chopped
- 2 tablespoons olive oil
- 4 cloves garlic, minced
- Salt and pepper to taste
- Red pepper flakes for garnish (optional)

DIRECTIONS:

1. In a large skillet, heat olive oil over medium heat. Add minced garlic and cook until fragrant.
2. Add chopped kale leaves to the skillet. Cook, stirring occasionally, until kale is wilted and tender.
3. Season with salt and pepper to taste.
4. Sprinkle with red pepper flakes for a bit of heat, if desired.
5. Serve the sautéed garlic kale hot.

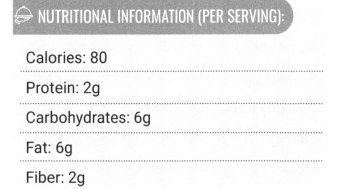

NUTRITIONAL INFORMATION (PER SERVING):

Calories: 100

Protein: 5g

Carbohydrates: 10g

Fat: 7g

Fiber: 4g

12. Lemon Herb Roasted Zucchini

INGREDIENTS:

- 2 medium zucchini, sliced into rounds
- 2 tablespoons olive oil
- Zest and juice of 1 lemon
- 1 tablespoon chopped fresh parsley
- 1 tablespoon chopped fresh basil
- Salt and pepper to taste

DIRECTIONS:

1. Preheat the oven to 400°F (200°C). Line a baking sheet with parchment paper.
2. In a large bowl, toss zucchini rounds with olive oil, lemon zest, lemon juice, chopped fresh parsley, chopped fresh basil, salt, and pepper until evenly coated.
3. Spread the seasoned zucchini rounds in a single layer on the prepared baking sheet.
4. Roast in the preheated oven for 15-20 minutes, or until the zucchini is tender and lightly browned.
5. Remove from the oven and serve hot.

NUTRITIONAL INFORMATION (PER SERVING):

Calories: 80

Protein: 2g

Carbohydrates: 6g

Fat: 6g

Fiber: 2g

13. Ginger Garlic Green Beans

INGREDIENTS:

- 1 pound green beans, trimmed
- 2 tablespoons olive oil
- 2 cloves garlic, minced
- 1 tablespoon grated ginger
- Salt and pepper to taste
- Sesame seeds for garnish (optional)

DIRECTIONS:

1. Steam green beans until tender-crisp, about 5 minutes. Drain and set aside.
2. In a large skillet, heat olive oil over medium heat. Add minced garlic and grated ginger. Cook until fragrant.
3. Add steamed green beans to the skillet. Cook for 2-3 minutes, tossing occasionally, until beans are coated in the ginger garlic mixture.
4. Season with salt and pepper to taste.
5. Sprinkle with sesame seeds before serving, if desired.

🍽 NUTRITIONAL INFORMATION (PER SERVING):

Calories: 80

Protein: 2g

Carbohydrates: 8g

Fat: 5g

Fiber: 3g

14. Lemon Herb Roasted Potatoes

INGREDIENTS:

- 1 pound baby potatoes, halved
- 2 tablespoons olive oil
- Zest and juice of 1 lemon
- 1 tablespoon chopped fresh rosemary
- 1 tablespoon chopped fresh thyme
- Salt and pepper to taste

DIRECTIONS:

1. Preheat the oven to 425°F (220°C). Line a baking sheet with parchment paper.
2. In a large bowl, toss halved baby potatoes with olive oil, lemon zest, lemon juice, chopped fresh rosemary, chopped fresh thyme, salt, and pepper until evenly coated.
3. Spread the seasoned potatoes in a single layer on the prepared baking sheet.
4. Roast in the preheated oven for 25-30 minutes, or until the potatoes are tender and golden brown.
5. Remove from the oven and serve hot.

🍽 NUTRITIONAL INFORMATION (PER SERVING):

Calories: 150

Protein: 3g

Carbohydrates: 20g

Fat: 7g

Fiber: 3g

15. Turmeric Roasted Cauliflower

INGREDIENTS:

- 1 head cauliflower, cut into florets
- 2 tablespoons olive oil
- 1 teaspoon ground turmeric
- 1 teaspoon ground cumin
- Salt and pepper to taste

DIRECTIONS:

1. Preheat the oven to 400°F (200°C). Line a baking sheet with parchment paper.
2. In a large bowl, toss cauliflower florets with olive oil, ground turmeric, ground cumin, salt, and pepper until evenly coated.
3. Spread the seasoned cauliflower in a single layer on the prepared baking sheet.
4. Roast in the preheated oven for 20-25 minutes, or until the cauliflower is tender and lightly browned.
5. Remove from the oven and serve hot.

NUTRITIONAL INFORMATION (PER SERVING):

Calories: 100	
Protein: 3g	
Carbohydrates: 8g	
Fat: 7g	
Fiber: 4g	

16. Garlic Herb Roasted Brussels Sprouts

INGREDIENTS:

- 1 pound Brussels sprouts, trimmed and halved
- 2 tablespoons olive oil
- 4 cloves garlic, minced
- 1 tablespoon chopped fresh rosemary
- 1 tablespoon chopped fresh thyme
- Salt and pepper to taste

DIRECTIONS:

1. Preheat the oven to 400°F (200°C). Line a baking sheet with parchment paper.
2. In a large bowl, toss halved Brussels sprouts with olive oil, minced garlic, chopped fresh rosemary, chopped fresh thyme, salt, and pepper until evenly coated.
3. Spread the seasoned Brussels sprouts in a single layer on the prepared baking sheet.
4. Roast in the preheated oven for 25-30 minutes, or until the Brussels sprouts are tender and caramelized.
5. Remove from the oven and serve hot.

NUTRITIONAL INFORMATION (PER SERVING):

Calories: 100	
Protein: 4g	
Carbohydrates: 12g	
Fat: 5g	
Fiber: 4g	

CHAPTER 14
RECIPES FOR 60 DAYS WEEKLY MEAL PLAN

WEEK 1: INTRODUCTION TO WHOLE FOODS

Breakfast: Oatmeal topped with Fresh Berries and a Sprinkle of Flaxseed

INGREDIENTS:

- 1/2 cup old-fashioned oats
- 1 cup water or milk of your choice
- Fresh berries (strawberries, blueberries, raspberries)
- 1 tablespoon ground flaxseed
- Optional: honey or maple syrup for sweetness

DIRECTIONS:

1. In a small saucepan, bring the water or milk to a boil.
2. Stir in the oats and reduce the heat to medium-low.
3. Cook the oats, stirring occasionally, for about 5 minutes or until they reach your desired consistency.
4. Transfer the cooked oatmeal to a bowl.
5. Top the oatmeal with fresh berries and sprinkle with ground flaxseed.
6. If desired, drizzle with honey or maple syrup for sweetness.
7. Serve hot and enjoy a nutritious start to your day!

Lunch: Grilled Chicken Salad with Mixed Greens, Vegetables, and Olive Oil Dressing

INGREDIENTS:

- 4 oz chicken breast, grilled and sliced
- Mixed salad greens (spinach, arugula, romaine lettuce)
- Assorted vegetables (cucumber, cherry tomatoes, bell peppers, red onion)
- 1 tablespoon olive oil
- 1 tablespoon balsamic vinegar
- Salt and pepper to taste

DIRECTIONS:

1. Prepare the grilled chicken breast by seasoning it with salt and pepper, then grilling until cooked through. Slice the grilled chicken into strips.
2. In a large bowl, combine the mixed salad greens and assorted vegetables.
3. Arrange the grilled chicken strips on top of the salad.
4. In a small bowl, whisk together the olive oil and balsamic vinegar to make the dressing.
5. Drizzle the dressing over the salad.
6. Toss the salad gently to coat everything with the dressing.
7. Serve immediately and enjoy a flavorful and satisfying lunch!

Dinner: Baked Salmon with Quinoa and Steamed Broccoli

INGREDIENTS:

- 4 oz salmon fillet
- 1/2 cup quinoa, rinsed
- 1 cup water or broth
- 1 cup broccoli florets
- Olive oil
- Salt and pepper to taste
- Lemon wedges for serving

DIRECTIONS:

1. Preheat the oven to 375°F (190°C).
2. Place the salmon fillet on a baking sheet lined with parchment paper.
3. Drizzle the salmon with olive oil and season with salt and pepper to taste.
4. Bake the salmon in the preheated oven for 12-15 minutes, or until cooked through and flaky.
5. While the salmon is baking, prepare the quinoa according to package instructions, using water or broth for cooking.
6. In a separate pot, steam the broccoli florets until tender.
7. Once everything is cooked, divide the quinoa, steamed broccoli, and baked salmon onto plates.
8. Serve with lemon wedges for squeezing over the salmon.
9. Enjoy a wholesome and nutritious dinner that's rich in protein, fiber, and healthy fats!

Snacks: Carrot Sticks with Hummus, Apple Slices with Almond Butter

INGREDIENTS:

- Carrot sticks
- Hummus
- Apple, sliced
- Almond butter

DIRECTIONS:

1. Wash and peel the carrots, then cut them into sticks.
2. Serve the carrot sticks with hummus for dipping.
3. Slice the apple into thin wedges.
4. Spread almond butter on the apple slices.
5. Enjoy these nutritious snacks between meals to keep hunger at bay and provide a boost of energy!

WEEK 2: INCORPORATING ANTI-INFLAMMATORY FATS

Breakfast: Anti-Inflammatory Green Smoothie

INGREDIENTS:

- 1 cup spinach leaves
- 1/2 ripe avocado
- 1 ripe banana
- 1 tablespoon chia seeds
- 1 cup almond milk (or any milk of your choice)
- Optional: honey or maple syrup for sweetness

DIRECTIONS:

1. Combine spinach, avocado, banana, chia seeds, and almond milk in a blender.
2. Blend until smooth and creamy.
3. Taste and add honey or maple syrup if desired for sweetness.
4. Pour into a glass and enjoy your nutritious and anti-inflammatory green smoothie!

Lunch: Turkey and Avocado Wrap

INGREDIENTS:

- 4 oz cooked turkey breast, sliced
- 1/2 avocado, sliced
- 1 whole grain tortilla
- Handful of mixed greens (spinach, arugula, lettuce)
- Hummus or Greek yogurt spread (optional)

DIRECTIONS:

1. Lay the whole grain tortilla flat on a clean surface.
2. Spread hummus or Greek yogurt over the tortilla, if desired.
3. Arrange sliced turkey breast, avocado, and mixed greens on top of the tortilla.
4. Roll the tortilla tightly into a wrap.
5. Cut the wrap in half diagonally.
6. Serve immediately or wrap it up for later, and enjoy a satisfying and anti-inflammatory lunch!

Dinner: Grilled Mackerel with Sweet Potato and Sauteed Kale

INGREDIENTS:

- 4 oz mackerel fillet
- 1 medium sweet potato, sliced
- 1 cup kale, chopped
- Olive oil
- Salt and pepper to taste
- Lemon wedges for serving

DIRECTIONS:

1. Preheat the grill or grill pan to medium-high heat.
2. Brush both sides of the mackerel fillet with olive oil and season with salt and pepper.
3. Grill the mackerel fillet for 3-4 minutes on each side, or until cooked through and flaky.
4. Meanwhile, lightly coat sweet potato slices with olive oil, salt, and pepper. Grill until tender, about 5-7 minutes per side.
5. In a separate skillet, heat olive oil over medium heat. Add chopped kale and sauté until wilted.
6. Serve the grilled mackerel with sweet potato slices, sautéed kale, and lemon wedges on the side.
7. Enjoy a delicious and anti-inflammatory dinner that's packed with omega-3 fatty acids and nutrient-rich vegetables!

Snacks: Walnuts, Greek Yogurt with Honey and Almonds

INGREDIENTS:

- Walnuts
- Greek yogurt
- Honey
- Almonds

DIRECTIONS:

1. Serve a handful of walnuts as a nutritious snack.
2. Enjoy a serving of Greek yogurt topped with honey and sliced almonds for extra flavor and crunch.
3. These snacks provide a healthy dose of protein, fiber, and healthy fats to keep you satisfied between meals while supporting an anti-inflammatory diet.

Breakfast: High-Fiber Cereal with Almond Milk and Sliced Banana

INGREDIENTS:

- 1 cup high-fiber cereal (look for varieties with whole grains and seeds)
- 1/2 cup unsweetened almond milk
- 1 ripe banana, sliced

DIRECTIONS:

1. Pour the high-fiber cereal into a bowl.
2. Add unsweetened almond milk over the cereal.
3. Top with sliced banana.
4. Enjoy this fiber-rich and anti-inflammatory breakfast to start your day off right!

Lunch: Lentil Soup with Side Salad and Whole Grain Roll

INGREDIENTS:

Ingredients for Lentil Soup:
- 1 cup dried lentils, rinsed and drained
- 4 cups vegetable broth
- 1 onion, chopped
- 2 carrots, diced
- 2 celery stalks, diced
- 2 cloves garlic, minced
- 1 teaspoon ground cumin
- 1 teaspoon ground turmeric
- Salt and pepper to taste
- Fresh parsley for garnish (optional)

Ingredients for Side Salad:
- Mixed salad greens (spinach, arugula, lettuce)
- Assorted vegetables (tomatoes, cucumbers, bell peppers)
- Balsamic vinaigrette dressing (optional)

Ingredients for Whole Grain Roll:
- 1 whole grain roll

DIRECTIONS:

1. In a large pot, combine the lentils, vegetable broth, chopped onion, diced carrots, diced celery, minced garlic, ground cumin, and ground turmeric.
2. Bring the mixture to a boil, then reduce the heat to low and let simmer for 25-30 minutes, or until the lentils are tender.
3. Season the lentil soup with salt and pepper to taste.
4. Ladle the lentil soup into bowls and garnish with fresh parsley, if desired.
5. Serve the lentil soup with a side salad and a whole grain roll for a satisfying and anti-inflammatory lunch.

Dinner: Stir-Fried Tofu with Mixed Vegetables and Brown Rice

INGREDIENTS:

- 8 oz firm tofu, drained and cubed
- 2 cups mixed vegetables (such as bell peppers, broccoli, snap peas, carrots)
- 2 tablespoons low-sodium soy sauce or tamari
- 1 tablespoon sesame oil
- 2 cloves garlic, minced
- 1 teaspoon grated ginger
- Cooked brown rice for serving

DIRECTIONS:

1. Heat sesame oil in a large skillet or wok over medium-high heat.
2. Add minced garlic and grated ginger to the skillet and cook until fragrant, about 1 minute.
3. Add cubed tofu to the skillet and stir-fry until golden brown on all sides, about 5-7 minutes.
4. Add mixed vegetables to the skillet and stir-fry until crisp-tender, about 3-5 minutes.
5. Pour low-sodium soy sauce or tamari over the tofu and vegetables, and stir to combine.
6. Serve the stir-fried tofu and mixed vegetables over cooked brown rice.
7. Enjoy this flavorful and nutritious dinner that's packed with plant-based protein and vibrant vegetables.

Snacks: Kefir, Sliced Pear with Cottage Cheese

INGREDIENTS:

- Kefir
- 1 ripe pear, sliced
- Cottage cheese

DIRECTIONS:

1. Enjoy a serving of kefir as a probiotic-rich snack.
2. Serve sliced pear with cottage cheese for a satisfying and anti-inflammatory snack option.

Breakfast: Greek Yogurt with Mixed Berries and Unsweetened Granola

INGREDIENTS:

- 1/2 cup Greek yogurt
- 1/2 cup mixed berries (strawberries, blueberries, raspberries)
- 2 tablespoons unsweetened granola

DIRECTIONS:

1. Spoon Greek yogurt into a bowl.
2. Top with mixed berries and unsweetened granola.
3. Enjoy this protein-packed and antioxidant-rich breakfast to start your day.

Lunch: Grilled Chicken Caesar Salad (No Croutons) with Vinaigrette Dressing

INGREDIENTS:

- 4 oz grilled chicken breast, sliced
- Mixed salad greens (romaine lettuce, kale, spinach)
- Cherry tomatoes, halved
- Parmesan cheese, shaved
- Vinaigrette dressing (olive oil, lemon juice, Dijon mustard, garlic, salt, and pepper)

DIRECTIONS:

1. In a large bowl, combine mixed salad greens and cherry tomatoes.
2. Top with sliced grilled chicken breast.
3. Drizzle vinaigrette dressing over the salad.
4. Garnish with shaved Parmesan cheese.
5. Toss gently to combine.
6. Enjoy this flavorful and nutrient-packed salad for lunch.

Dinner: Beef Stir-Fry with Bell Peppers, Broccoli, and Quinoa

INGREDIENTS:

- 8 oz beef, thinly sliced
- 1 bell pepper, sliced
- 1 cup broccoli florets
- 2 cloves garlic, minced
- 2 tablespoons low-sodium soy sauce or tamari
- 1 tablespoon sesame oil
- Cooked quinoa for serving

DIRECTIONS:

1. Heat sesame oil in a large skillet or wok over medium-high heat.
2. Add minced garlic to the skillet and cook until fragrant, about 1 minute.
3. Add sliced beef to the skillet and stir-fry until browned, about 3-4 minutes.
4. Add bell pepper slices and broccoli florets to the skillet and continue to stir-fry until vegetables are crisp-tender, about 3-5 minutes.
5. Pour low-sodium soy sauce or tamari over the beef and vegetables, and stir to combine.
6. Serve the beef stir-fry over cooked quinoa.
7. Enjoy this delicious and nutritious dinner that's rich in protein and colorful vegetables.

Snacks: Sliced Cucumber with Guacamole, Fresh Cherries

INGREDIENTS:

- Cucumber, sliced
- Guacamole
- Fresh cherries

DIRECTIONS:

1. Serve sliced cucumber with guacamole for a refreshing and nutrient-rich snack.
2. Enjoy fresh cherries as a sweet and antioxidant-packed snack option.

Breakfast: Vegetable Omelet with Spinach, Tomatoes, and Onions

INGREDIENTS:

- 2 eggs
- Handful of spinach leaves
- 1/2 tomato, diced
- 1/4 onion, diced
- Salt and pepper to taste
- Olive oil or cooking spray for the pan

DIRECTIONS:

1. In a bowl, whisk together the eggs until well beaten. Season with salt and pepper.
2. Heat a non-stick skillet over medium heat and lightly coat with olive oil or cooking spray.
3. Add diced onion to the skillet and sauté until softened, about 2 minutes.
4. Add diced tomato and spinach leaves to the skillet and cook until spinach is wilted, about 1-2 minutes.
5. Pour beaten eggs into the skillet, covering the vegetables evenly.
6. Cook the omelet until the bottom is set and the edges are slightly browned, about 2-3 minutes.
7. Carefully flip the omelet and cook for another 1-2 minutes until cooked through.
8. Slide the omelet onto a plate and fold it in half.
9. Serve hot and enjoy a nutritious and satisfying breakfast!

Lunch: Quinoa Salad with Beets, Carrots, and Lemon-Olive Oil Dressing

INGREDIENTS:

- 1 cup cooked quinoa
- 1 small beet, cooked and diced
- 1 carrot, shredded
- Handful of mixed salad greens
- 2 tablespoons lemon juice
- 1 tablespoon extra virgin olive oil
- Salt and pepper to taste

DIRECTIONS:

1. In a large bowl, combine cooked quinoa, diced beet, shredded carrot, and mixed salad greens.
2. In a small bowl, whisk together lemon juice, extra virgin olive oil, salt, and pepper to make the dressing.
3. Pour the dressing over the quinoa salad and toss until well combined.
4. Serve immediately or refrigerate until ready to eat.
5. Enjoy this colorful and nutrient-rich quinoa salad for lunch!

Dinner: Baked Cod with Mixed Roasted Vegetables

INGREDIENTS:

- 8 oz cod fillet
- Assorted vegetables (bell peppers, zucchini, cherry tomatoes, red onion)
- Olive oil
- Salt and pepper to taste
- Lemon wedges for serving

DIRECTIONS:

1. Preheat the oven to 400°F (200°C).
2. Place the cod fillet on a baking sheet lined with parchment paper.
3. Drizzle olive oil over the cod fillet and season with salt and pepper.
4. Arrange the assorted vegetables around the cod fillet on the baking sheet.
5. Drizzle olive oil over the vegetables and season with salt and pepper.
6. Bake in the preheated oven for 15-20 minutes, or until the cod is cooked through and flakes easily with a fork.
7. Remove from the oven and squeeze lemon wedges over the cod and vegetables.
8. Serve hot and enjoy a flavorful and nutritious dinner!

Snacks: Mixed Berries, Bell Pepper Slices with Hummus

INGREDIENTS:

- Mixed berries (strawberries, blueberries, raspberries)
- Bell pepper, sliced
- Hummus

DIRECTIONS:

1. Enjoy a handful of mixed berries as a refreshing and antioxidant-rich snack.
2. Serve bell pepper slices with hummus for a satisfying and nutritious snack option.

Breakfast: Turmeric and Ginger-Infused Oatmeal with Apple Slices

INGREDIENTS:

- 1/2 cup rolled oats
- 1 cup water or milk of choice
- 1/2 teaspoon ground turmeric
- 1/2 teaspoon ground ginger
- 1 small apple, sliced
- Optional toppings: honey, maple syrup, or nuts

DIRECTIONS:

1. In a small saucepan, combine rolled oats, water or milk, ground turmeric, and ground ginger.
2. Bring the mixture to a boil over medium heat, then reduce the heat to low and simmer for about 5 minutes, stirring occasionally, until the oats are cooked and creamy.
3. Remove from heat and let it sit for a minute to thicken.
4. Serve the turmeric and ginger-infused oatmeal in a bowl, topped with sliced apple.
5. Optional: drizzle with honey, maple syrup, or sprinkle with nuts for added sweetness and crunch.
6. Enjoy this warm and comforting breakfast packed with anti-inflammatory spices and fruits!

Lunch: Chicken Curry with Mixed Vegetables and Basmati Rice

INGREDIENTS:

- 4 oz chicken breast, diced
- 1/2 cup mixed vegetables (such as bell peppers, carrots, peas)
- 1/4 cup coconut milk
- 2 tablespoons curry powder
- Cooked basmati rice for serving
- Olive oil
- Salt and pepper to taste

DIRECTIONS:

1. Heat olive oil in a skillet over medium heat. Add diced chicken breast and cook until browned and cooked through.
2. Add mixed vegetables to the skillet and cook until softened.
3. Stir in curry powder and cook for another minute until fragrant.
4. Pour coconut milk into the skillet and stir to combine. Simmer for a few minutes until the sauce thickens.
5. Season with salt and pepper to taste.
6. Serve the chicken curry over cooked basmati rice.
7. Enjoy this flavorful and aromatic lunch that's packed with protein and vegetables!

Dinner: Turkey Chili with Beans and Cumin

INGREDIENTS:

- 1 lb lean ground turkey
- 1 can (15 oz) kidney beans, drained and rinsed
- 1 can (15 oz) black beans, drained and rinsed
- 1 can (14.5 oz) diced tomatoes
- 1 onion, chopped
- 2 cloves garlic, minced
- 1 tablespoon ground cumin
- Salt and pepper to taste
- Olive oil

DIRECTIONS:

1. Heat olive oil in a large pot over medium heat. Add chopped onion and minced garlic, and cook until softened.
2. Add ground turkey to the pot and cook until browned, breaking it up with a spoon.
3. Stir in ground cumin, salt, and pepper.
4. Add diced tomatoes, kidney beans, and black beans to the pot. Bring to a simmer.
5. Reduce heat to low and let the chili simmer for about 20-25 minutes, stirring occasionally.
6. Taste and adjust seasoning if necessary.
7. Serve hot and enjoy this hearty and flavorful turkey chili!

Snacks: Cinnamon-Spiced Almonds, Sliced Pineapple

INGREDIENTS:

- Almonds
- Ground cinnamon
- Pineapple, sliced

DIRECTIONS:

1. Toss almonds with ground cinnamon until evenly coated.
2. Roast the cinnamon-spiced almonds in the oven at 350°F (175°C) for about 10-12 minutes, or until fragrant and lightly toasted.
3. Let the almonds cool before enjoying as a crunchy and satisfying snack.
4. Enjoy sliced pineapple as a sweet and refreshing snack option.

Breakfast: Chia Pudding with Mixed Fruit and Honey

INGREDIENTS:

- 2 tablespoons chia seeds
- 1/2 cup unsweetened almond milk (or any milk of choice)
- Mixed fruit (such as strawberries, blueberries, raspberries)
- Honey for drizzling

DIRECTIONS:

1. In a bowl or jar, mix together chia seeds and almond milk.
2. Stir well to combine and let it sit in the refrigerator for at least 2 hours or overnight to thicken.
3. Once the chia pudding has thickened, layer it with mixed fruit in a serving bowl or glass.
4. Drizzle honey over the top for sweetness.
5. Serve chilled and enjoy a nutritious and delicious breakfast!

Lunch: Grilled Salmon Salad with Fresh Greens and Cucumber

INGREDIENTS:

- 4 oz salmon fillet
- Mixed salad greens (spinach, arugula, lettuce)
- 1/2 cucumber, sliced
- Olive oil
- Lemon juice
- Salt and pepper to taste

DIRECTIONS:

1. Preheat the grill or grill pan over medium-high heat.
2. Brush olive oil over the salmon fillet and season with salt and pepper.
3. Grill the salmon fillet for 3-4 minutes on each side, or until cooked through and flaky.
4. In a large bowl, toss mixed salad greens and sliced cucumber with olive oil and lemon juice.
5. Divide the salad onto plates and top with grilled salmon fillet.
6. Serve immediately and enjoy a light and refreshing grilled salmon salad for lunch!

Dinner: Roasted Chicken with Asparagus and Sweet Potatoes

INGREDIENTS:

- 4 chicken thighs, bone-in and skin-on
- 1 bunch asparagus, trimmed
- 2 sweet potatoes, peeled and diced
- Olive oil
- Salt and pepper to taste
- Herbs (such as rosemary, thyme, or parsley) for garnish

DIRECTIONS:

1. Preheat the oven to 400°F (200°C).
2. Place chicken thighs on a baking sheet lined with parchment paper. Drizzle with olive oil and season with salt and pepper.
3. Arrange trimmed asparagus and diced sweet potatoes around the chicken thighs on the baking sheet. Drizzle with olive oil and season with salt and pepper.
4. Roast in the preheated oven for 25-30 minutes, or until the chicken is cooked through and the vegetables are tender and lightly browned.
5. Remove from the oven and let it rest for a few minutes.
6. Garnish with herbs before serving.
7. Serve hot and enjoy a hearty and nutritious roasted chicken with asparagus and sweet potatoes for dinner!

Snacks: Sliced Watermelon, Celery Sticks with Almond Butter

INGREDIENTS:

- Watermelon, sliced
- Celery sticks
- Almond butter

DIRECTIONS:

1. Enjoy slices of watermelon as a hydrating and refreshing snack.
2. Serve celery sticks with almond butter for a satisfying and nutritious snack option.

- **Breakfast:** Your favorite breakfast from the past seven weeks.
- **Lunch:** Your favorite lunch from the past seven weeks.
- **Dinner:** Your favorite dinner from the past seven weeks.
- **Snacks:** Your favorite snacks from the past seven weeks.

CHAPTER 15
SUCCESS STORIES AND INSPIRATIONS

Success Story 1: Emily's Journey to Wellness

Emily, a 35-year-old graphic designer, struggled with chronic joint pain and fatigue for years. Her days were marked by discomfort, making her personal and professional life challenging. After numerous doctor visits, Emily was advised to try an anti-inflammatory diet as a holistic approach to her symptoms.

Skeptical but desperate for relief, Emily started eliminating processed foods, sugars, and red meat from her diet, replacing them with leafy greens, nuts, and fatty fish rich in Omega-3s. The change didn't happen overnight, but within a few weeks, Emily started noticing a significant reduction in her pain and an increase in energy.

Three months into her new diet, Emily felt like a new person. She was not only pain-free but also had more vitality and clarity than she had in years. Inspired by her own success, Emily began sharing her journey on social media, motivating others to consider dietary changes for chronic inflammation.

Success Story 2: Mark's Weight Loss and Inflammation Control

Mark, a 50-year-old teacher, faced a wake-up call during a routine check-up: his weight was creeping up, and his blood tests showed high levels of inflammation markers. Concerned about his health and the risk of chronic diseases, Mark decided it was time for a change.

He consulted with a nutritionist and started following an anti-inflammatory diet, cutting out sugary drinks, fried foods, and processed carbohydrates. Instead, he focused on whole foods, such as berries, green vegetables, and lean proteins.

Six months later, not only had Mark lost 40 pounds, but his inflammation levels had drastically decreased, leading to better overall health and reduced risk of diseases associated with chronic inflammation, such as heart disease and diabetes. Mark's story became a testament to the power of dietary changes in combating inflammation and promoting a healthier lifestyle.

Success Story 3: Anna's Battle Against Skin Conditions

Anna, a 28-year-old software developer, had been battling severe eczema and psoriasis since her teenage years. The constant itch and visible red patches made her self-conscious and affected her social life. After trying countless creams and medications with little to no long-term success, Anna felt defeated.

Her turning point came when a friend suggested trying an anti-inflammatory diet, highlighting the potential impact of diet on skin health. Skeptical but desperate for a solution, Anna decided to give it a shot. She eliminated gluten, dairy, and refined sugars from her diet, instead focusing on anti-inflammatory foods like turmeric, blueberries, and leafy greens.

The results were beyond her expectations. Within weeks, Anna noticed a significant decrease in redness and irritation. Months into her new diet, her skin was clearer than it had been in over a decade. Encouraged by her results, Anna started a blog to share her journey and recipes, becoming an inspiration to others suffering from similar skin conditions.

Success Story 4: David's Fight Against Chronic Fatigue and Depression

David, a 42-year-old school principal, had been dealing with unexplained chronic fatigue and mild depression. Despite his active lifestyle and healthy eating habits, he couldn't shake off the perpetual state of tiredness and low mood.

After extensive research, David stumbled upon information linking chronic inflammation to fatigue and depression. Intrigued, he decided to adjust his diet to combat inflammation. He increased his intake of fatty fish, whole grains, and antioxidants, while reducing his consumption of processed foods and sugars.

The impact was life-changing. Within a few months, David's energy levels soared, and his mood improved significantly. His newfound vitality allowed him to engage more actively with his family and students. Inspired by his own transformation, David began organizing workshops for his staff and students on the importance of diet in managing stress and enhancing mental well-being.

David's story highlights the often-overlooked connection between diet, mental health, and physical well-being. His success serves as a beacon of hope for those struggling with similar issues, proving that dietary changes can lead to profound improvements in quality of life.

Inspirations: The Community's Collective Journey

The success stories of individuals like Emily and Mark have sparked a movement within their community. Local groups started forming to support each other in adopting an anti-inflammatory diet. These groups share recipes, success stories, and tips for maintaining this healthier lifestyle.

The community's collective journey has shown that while individual experiences vary, the positive impact of an anti-inflammatory diet on health and well-being is undeniable. It's a reminder that with the right support and commitment, anyone can take control of their health and find relief from chronic inflammation.

CONCLUSION

As we reach the end of our journey through the world of the anti-inflammatory diet, we hope that this book has provided you with not only a deeper understanding of the science behind inflammation and how it affects our body but also a practical guide to combatting it through diet.

From the initial exploration of what constitutes an anti-inflammatory diet in Chapter 1, to the detailed 60-day meal plan preparations in Chapter 3, this guide has been designed to ease you into a lifestyle that can significantly improve your health and well-being. The variety of recipes from breakfast to dinner, salads to soups, and desserts to vegetarian dishes, as outlined in Chapters 4 through 13, are meant to cater to diverse tastes and dietary needs, ensuring that everyone can find something suitable to incorporate into their daily lives.

Furthermore, the inspiring success stories in Chapter 15 serve as a testament to the transformative power of mindful eating. These narratives not only provide motivation but also affirm the positive outcomes that come from dedication and change.

In conclusion, this book is not just a collection of recipes; it is a roadmap to a healthier, more vibrant life. It is our hope that the principles and practices laid out in these pages will inspire you to embrace the anti-inflammatory diet as a sustainable lifestyle change. Remember, the journey to better health is a marathon, not a sprint. Start small, be consistent, and let the positive changes unfold.

Thank you for choosing this path to wellness. Here's to your health, happiness, and a life free from the clutches of chronic inflammation.

Index

Made in the USA
Coppell, TX
08 May 2024

32144112R10070